Catechumenal Pathways for Married Life

CATECHUMENAL PATHWAYS FOR MARRIED LIFE

Pastoral guidelines for local Churches

DICASTERY OF LAITY, FAMILY AND LIFE

PREFACE BY POPE FRANCIS

Our Sunday Visitor
Huntington, Indiana

Our Sunday Visitor Publishing Division
Our Sunday Visitor, Inc.
200 Noll Plaza
Huntington, IN 46750
1-800-348-2440

ISBN: 978-1-63966-106-0 (Inventory No. T2833)
eISBN: 978-1-63966-107-7
LCCN: 2023936226
Cover design: Tyler Ottinger
Cover art: AdobeStock
Interior design: Amanda Falk

PRINTED IN THE UNITED STATES OF AMERICA

TABLE OF CONTENTS

Preface

"The Christian proclamation on the family is good news indeed" (*Amoris Laetitia*, 1). This affirmation from the *relatio finalis* of the Synod of Bishops on the Family offered a worthy opening for the apostolic exhortation *Amoris Laetitia*. For the Church, in every age, is called to proclaim anew the beauty and abundance of grace contained in the Sacrament of Matrimony and family life which flows from it, especially to young people. Five years after its publication, the *Amoris Laetitia* Family Year sought to return our focus to the family, to invite us to reflect on the themes of the apostolic exhortation, and to enliven the entire Church in her joyful commitment to evangelize families, alongside families.

One of the fruits of this special year are the "Catechumenal Pathways for Married Life," which I now have the pleasure of entrusting to pastors, spouses, and all those who provide pastoral care for families. This pastoral tool was prepared by the Dicastery for Laity, Family, and Life, in response to a request I have repeatedly expressed — namely, "the need for a 'new catechumenate' for marriage preparation." Indeed, "it is urgent to effectively implement what has already been proposed in *Familiaris Consortio* (no. 66). Just as the catechumenate is part of the sacramental process for the baptism of adults, so, too, may the preparation for marriage form an integral part of the whole sacramental procedure of marriage, as an antidote to prevent the increase of invalid or inconsistent marriage celebrations" (*Address to the Roman Rota*, January 21, 2017).

Emerging here, in no uncertain terms, was a serious concern that couples who receive a superficial preparation run the real risk of celebrating a marriage which is null and void, or one with such a weak foundation that it "falls apart" in a short space of time and cannot withstand even the first inevitable crisis. These marriage failures bring with them great suffering and leave deep wounds in people. They become disillusioned, bitter, and, in the most painful cases, even end up no longer believing in the vocation to love, inscribed by God himself in the heart of the human being. Therefore, we have a primary duty to responsibly accompany those who manifest their intention to be united in marriage, so that they may be preserved from the trauma of separation and never lose faith in love.

However, a desire for justice should also animate us. The Church is mother, and a mother does not play favorites among her children. She does not treat them with disparity; she gives each an equal dose of care, attention, and time. Devoting time to someone is a sign of love: If we do not devote time to a person, it is a sign that we do not love them. This truth often comes to my mind when I consider that the Church devotes large quantities of time — several years — to the preparation of candidates for the priesthood or religious life, but devotes very little time — only a few weeks — to those preparing for marriage. Like priests and consecrated persons, married couples are also children of Mother Church, and such a vast divergence in treatment is unjust. Married couples constitute the vast majority of the faithful, and they are often pillars of support in parishes, volunteer groups, associations, and movements. They are truly "guardians of life," not only because they beget children, educate them, and accompany their growth, but also because they care for the elderly in their family, and devote themselves to the service of people with disabilities and frequently to people living in poverty with whom they come into contact. Vocations to the priesthood and consecrated life grow out of families, and it is families that make up the fabric of society and "mend its tears" with patience and daily sacrifices. Mother Church therefore bears a duty of justice to devote time and energy to the preparation of those whom the Lord calls to the great mission of family life.

Therefore, in order to give concrete form to this urgent need, "I recommended the implementation of a true catechumenate for future spouses including all the steps of the sacramental path: time of preparation for marriage, its celebration, and the years immediately thereafter" (*Address to Participants in the Course on the Marriage Process*, February 25, 2017). This is exactly what the document I present here seeks to do and for which I am grateful. It is structured according to three phases: preparation for marriage (remote, proximate, and final); the celebration of the wedding; the accompaniment during the first years of married life. As can be seen, the goal is to walk an important stretch of road together with couples in the journey of life, even after the wedding, especially during moments of crisis or discouragement. In this way, we will try to be faithful to the Church, which is mother, teacher, and traveling companion, always at our side.

It is my fervent desire that this first document be followed as soon as possible by another one, which should offer concrete pastoral programs and options of pathways for accompaniment, and which should be specifically dedicated to those couples who have experienced the failure of their marriage and are living in a new union or are civilly remarried. Indeed, the Church desires to be close to these couples and to walk with them also, along the *via caritatis* (cf. *Amoris Laetitia*, 306), so that they never feel abandoned but can find communities that are accessible and fraternal places of welcome, as well as assistance in discernment and participation.

This first document is a gift as well as a responsibility. It is a gift, because it makes available to all abundant and stimulating material, which is the fruit of reflection and pastoral experiences already implemented in various dioceses/eparchies around the world. Yet, it is also a responsibility because it does not offer "magic formulas" that work automatically. It is a dress that must be "tailor-made" for the people who will wear it. The document offers guidelines that need to be welcomed, adapted, and put into practice in the concrete social, cultural, and ecclesial situations in which each particular Church lives. I appeal, therefore, to the docility, zeal, and creativity of the Church's pastors, and those who assist them, to increase the effectiveness of the vital and indispensable work of formation, proclamation, and accompaniment of families, which the Holy Spirit is asking us to carry out at this time.

"I did not at all shrink from telling you what was for your benefit, or from teaching you" (Acts 20:20). I urge all those who offer pastoral care to families to make these words of the apostle Paul their own and not to be discouraged in the face of a responsibility which may seem difficult, challenging, or even beyond our means. Be courageous! Let us begin to take the first steps. Let us initiate a process of pastoral renewal. Let us put our minds and hearts at the service of future families. I assure you that the Lord will sustain us, give us wisdom and strength, make our enthusiasm grow, and above all, allow us to experience the "delightful and comforting joy of evangelizing" (*Evangelii Gaudium*, 9) as we proclaim the Gospel of the family to new generations.

Franciscus

Introduction

The proposal of the Holy Father Francis for a "marriage catechumenate"

1. The Holy Father Francis has on several occasions expressed his desire for the Church to offer a better and more thorough preparation of young couples for marriage, insisting on the need for a relatively broad approach, inspired by the baptismal catechumenate, which would enable them to celebrate the Sacrament of Marriage with greater awareness, beginning with an experience of faith and personal encounter with Jesus.[1]

2. This document, which takes up a theme already explored in a document produced by the former Pontifical Council for the Family,[2] seeks to respond to this concern of the Holy Father and to support the local Churches in thinking about or rethinking their pathways to marriage preparation and pastoral accompaniment during the first years of married life. Therefore, these "pastoral guidelines" should not be understood — in neither form nor content — as a structured and complete premarital course which can readily be employed in ordinary pastoral care. Rather, their purpose is to set forth some general principles, as well as a concrete and comprehensive pastoral proposal, which each local Church is invited to consider in the elaboration of its own catechumenal pathway for married life, thus responding creatively to the Pope's appeal.[3]

3. The contemporary reality requires renewed pastoral efforts to strengthen preparation to the Sacrament of Marriage in dioceses/eparchies and parishes on all continents. The ever-diminishing number of people getting married in general, but especially the brief duration of marriages, even sacramental ones, as well as the problem of the validity of marriages celebrated, constitute an urgent challenge which puts at stake the personal fulfillment and happiness of a great many lay faithful around the world. An obvious fragility of marriage lies at the origin of many difficulties that families experience, which is in turn caused by a host of factors, including: a hedonistic mentality which distorts the beauty and depth of human sexuality; a self-centeredness which makes it difficult to espouse the commitments of married life; a limited understanding of the gift of the Sacrament of Marriage, the meaning of spousal love, and its essence as an authentic vocation, that is, a response to God's call to the man and woman who decide to marry, etc. The concern of Mother Church for her children in need of assistance and guidance should prompt her to invest new energies in favor of couples, "in order that their experience of love may become a sacrament, an efficacious sign of salvation."[4]

I. General Guidelines

Reasons for a catechumenate

4. The idea of creating *catechumenal pathways for married life* is not new in ecclesial reflection.[1] Following the two Synods on the Family in 2014 and 2015, Pope Francis called for such a proposal several times in his ordinary magisterium, and it has gradually taken shape in his pastoral reflection, offering outlines for a renewed journey of accompaniment on the path toward marriage.[2]

5. In the early Church — according to the shared conviction of the Church Fathers — a clear Christian orientation in life must precede the celebration of the sacrament. "One must first become a disciple of the Lord, and then be admitted to holy baptism," stated Saint Basil.[3] Faith and conversion were two unequivocal signs of such a new orientation of life. In fact, the ancient catechumenate was a time to form candidates for baptism by nurturing their faith and encouraging them to conversion. Faith opened the heart and mind to God and Jesus Christ's work of salvation; conversion sought to correct behaviors, habits, and life practices that were incompatible with the new Christian existence which the catechumens were about to embrace.

In a similar way to that which occurred before baptism in the early Church, a path of faith formation and accompaniment toward the acquisition of a Christian lifestyle — a path specifically intended for couples — would offer great assistance today in relation to the celebration of marriage.[4] Indeed, the catechumenate can inspire new methods for faith renewal in every age, because it proposes a type of accompaniment for people — pedagogical, gradual, and ritualized — which always retains its effectiveness. Specifically, the marriage catechumenate does not aim to be a simple catechesis, nor to transmit a doctrine. It aims to let the mystery of sacramental grace resonate among the spouses, since it belongs to them by virtue of the sacrament: It seeks to bring to life the presence of Christ in them and among them.[5] For this reason, the Church must go beyond a type of formation which is solely intellectual, theoretical, and general — that is, religious literacy — when engaging with those who intend to marry. We need to walk with them along a path that leads to an encounter with Christ, or to deepen this relationship, and assist them in making an authentic discernment of their own vocation to marriage, both on a personal and interpersonal level.[6]

Those responsible for this task

6. It is the duty of the entire ecclesial community to elaborate a catechumenal pathway for marriage preparation and to offer concrete accompaniment to couples along this path. The journey should be shared among priests, Christian spouses, religious men and women, and pastoral workers, who must collaborate among themselves and in agreement with their bishop. Marriage is not only a social act; for Christians, it is an "ecclesial" act. Therefore, the whole Church, as the body of Christ, takes charge of it, and feels the need to be of service to future families.[7]

7. The conviction from which to begin — for engaged couples preparing for marriage and for pastoral workers accompanying them — is that marriage is not a point of arrival: It is a vocation, a path to holiness that embraces a person's entire life.[8] Moreover, by virtue of their participation in the prophetic and royal priesthood of Christ, the lay faithful also receive a specific ecclesial mission in the Sacrament of Matrimony for which they need to be prepared and accompanied.[9] Therefore, just as the Church takes care to prepare priests and religious to live out their vocation and mission by devoting long years of formation to them, in the same way the Church has a duty to adequately prepare those lay faithful who feel called to accept the vocation of marriage and to persevere in it throughout their lives by carrying out the mission with which they have been invested.[10] The Sacrament of Holy Orders, religious consecration, and the Sacrament of Matrimony all deserve the same care, since the Lord calls men and women with the same intensity and love to one vocation or the other.

8. In order to effectively implement a renewed pastoral care of married life, it has now become indispensable that couples offering accompaniment, in parishes and family movements, as well as priests, already from the time of their seminary formation, and religious and consecrated men and women, be adequately formed and prepared in mutual complementarity and ecclesial co-responsibility.[11] This natural communion in the apostolate between spouses and consecrated celibates has been part of the Church's life since its very beginnings, as shown by the example of Paul who was assisted

in his evangelizing activities by Aquila and Priscilla.[12] However, that communion needs to be rediscovered and lived out fully today in parishes and at the diocesan level, because the diversity of approach and language, the diversity of life experiences, and the diversity of charisms and spiritual gifts proper to each vocation and state of life offer great enrichment in the transmission of the Faith to young couples and in their initiation into married life.

9. Those entrusted with pastoral ministry — parish priests, religious men and women, bishops — perform an important task of oversight and coordination.[13] In particular, priests and parish priests — usually the first to receive young people's request to marry in the Church — have a great responsibility to welcome, encourage, and deftly guide engaged couples, as well as to immediately impress upon them the profound religious dimension involved in Christian marriage, which is far superior to a simple "civil ceremony" or "matter of custom."[14]

10. Married couples must also play a primary role alongside priests and religious. The preparation of couples for marriage is a true work of evangelization,[15] and the lay faithful, especially married couples, receive an equally important call as religious and ordained ministers to participate in the Church's evangelizing mission: They are pastoral workers.[16] Because of their unique experience, they can offer concrete support along the journey of accompaniment by intervening as witnesses and companions of couples, both before and during mar-

riage, regarding many aspects of married life (emotional, sexual, communicational, and spiritual) and family life (duties of care and nurturing, openness to life, reciprocal self-offering, raising children, and mutual support in daily labors, difficulties, and illnesses). Spouses who make themselves available for this valuable service of accompaniment receive great benefit themselves. Indeed, carrying out a pastoral commitment together and proclaiming the "Gospel of marriage" to others helps deepen a couple's spiritual union, and enriches spouses both individually and as a couple. Nevertheless, lay people, particularly spouses as they live out this prominent ecclesial task, shall not replace the priest by taking on roles and tasks which are not proper to them. For their part, priests and religious shall take care not to limit the laity's contribution to that of mere bystanders, since lay faithful are entitled to effective co-responsibility. Priests and religious, therefore, shall seek to embrace an attitude of constant listening and verification of their journey together with the married couples who work with them and who live the familial dimension firsthand, while avoiding the risk of being the sole agents or, on the other hand, of making excessive requests or delegating unduly, thereby running the risk of "exhausting families."

Renewing pastoral care of married life

11. Therefore, the pastoral renewal requested by Pope Francis since the beginning of his pontificate[17] must also embrace the pastoral care of married life. In this field, the path of renewal can be traced out on the basis of three specific "principles": interconnectedness,

synodality, and continuity.

12. *Interconnectedness* means that the pastoral care of married life is not confined to the narrow arena of "meetings for engaged couples," but "crosses" into other pastoral areas, which always seek to include it. Such an approach can avoid an inflexible division of pastoral care into "watertight compartments," which diminish its effectiveness. Rather, pastoral care of children, young people, and families should all advance in tandem by working in synergy. Each field needs to be aware of the others' pastoral journey and goals in order to engender a linear growth process and a gradual deepening of faith. The pastor should play an important role by coordinating along with the pastoral team. Additionally, it would be of great benefit to always include in each of these three fields a *vocational perspective*, which unifies and gives consistency to people's faith and life journey. Even *social pastoral care* should be integrated with pastoral care of the family, since social pastoral care cannot be properly understood without "listening" to the family, just as the family cannot be understood without taking into account how they are affected by their contemporary social reality.

13. *Synodality* defines the specific *modus vivendi et operandi* of the Church. The Church is communion, and concretely fulfills its essence of communion by walking together, coordinating among all pastoral fields, and encouraging the active participation of all her members in the mission of evangelization.[18] The pastoral care of married life must also be carried out according

to this synodal key. It must be "taken on" by all within the Church in a co-responsible manner, must span all pastoral spheres, and must go hand in hand with the shared journey of the Church in every historical epoch, growing with her and being updated and renewed within her.

14. *Continuity* refers to the nature of pastoral care of married life, which is not "episodic" but "prolonged in time" — one might even say "permanent." Such an approach makes it possible to set up pedagogical pathways to accompany children and young people throughout their various stages of growth — on both human and faith levels — toward the gradual discovery of their vocation, whether it be to marriage, priesthood, or religious life. The marital vocation should therefore be rooted in the journey of Christian initiation into the Faith even from childhood.[19]

15. In light of these considerations, the Church needs to seriously rethink how she accompanies the human and spiritual growth of the faithful. Indeed, in many countries, the ordinary activity of parishes displays long periods of "pastoral abandonment" during certain moments in the lives of individuals and families, which unfortunately cause estrangement from the community and often also from the Faith. Think, for example, of the experience of parents after receiving catechesis before the baptism of their children, or of children after receiving their first Communion. In order to fill these "pastoral gaps," specific vocational programs should be considered as a way to continue offering basic catechet-

ical formation and other forms of accompaniment, so that parents can assist their children's spiritual growth during childhood and adolescence, and feel supported in this aim by a community with which they can share their reflections and experiences.[20]

II. A Concrete Proposal

16. Pope Francis has recommended "the implementation of a true catechumenate of future spouses including all the steps of the sacramental path: time of preparation for the marriage, its celebration, and the years immediately thereafter."[1] As already stated, each diocese/eparchy has the duty to work out, or rethink, its own marriage-preparation pathway inspired by the pre-baptismal catechumenate. Each program will have to consider the opportunities and limitations offered by the local geographical, cultural, and pastoral milieu, drawing from these guidelines in a flexible and creative way.

In developing this project, certain requirements will have to be taken into consideration:

- the program should last for a period of time sufficient to allow couples to truly reflect and mature;
- although beginning with the concrete experience of human love, faith and personal encounter with Christ should be placed at the center of marriage preparation;
- the program should be articulated in phases, and — where possible and appropriate — marked by rites of passage to be celebrated within the community;
- each of the following elements should be

included (without any exceptions): formation, reflection, discussion, dialogue, liturgy, community, prayer, and celebration.

However, even after a diocese/eparchy has developed its own marriage preparation pathway, this "pastoral tool" cannot simply be "imposed" as the only way to prepare for marriage. Rather, it should be used with discernment and common sense, with full awareness that there are cases in which the marriage catechumenate cannot or should not be followed, and that other ways and forms of preparation for marriage should be found.

Modalities

17. After creating its own form of marriage catechumenate, each diocese/eparchy should examine it closely during a period of experimentation and testing through a "pilot project," which should first be launched either in all or only in some parishes (depending on the pastoral context). After this initial experimentation, the opinions and evaluations of both pastoral workers and participating couples should be gathered, in order to reflect together on the strengths and shortcomings that will have arisen, before proceeding accordingly with the necessary adjustments.

18. When faced with the plurality of personal situations, each diocese/eparchy could plan a common form of catechumenal pathways and then evaluate ways to customize them according to the couples. Pastoral creativity and flexibility will be essential in order to embrace the concrete situation faced by various couples: reli-

gious practice, social and economic motivations, age, cohabitation, presence of children, and other factors related to the decision to marry.

19. The Order of Christian Initiation for Adults can offer a general framework for inspiration. It will be especially important to: give importance to what precedes and follows the catechumenate (initial evangelization and mystagogy, respectively); ensure that transitions from one period to another are marked by discernment, symbols, and rituals (in places where cultural considerations permit); and create a clear connection between the other sacraments (baptism, Eucharist, confirmation) and marriage. In all of this, it must be recalled that the act of imparting the Faith requires a personal encounter with Christ, conversion of heart in daily life, and the experience of the Spirit in ecclesial communion.

20. Those who accompany couples — married couples, presbyters, and pastoral workers in general — should possess a formation and style of accompaniment suited to the catechumenal journey. As already mentioned, it is not so much a matter of sharing notions or imparting skills. Rather, it is about guiding, assisting, and being close to couples along a path [so as] to walk together. The marriage catechumenate is not a preparation for an "exam to pass," but for a "life to live." Considering this goal, the ongoing formation and training of priests and religious should remain a priority, since they often use language that is "distant" from the concrete reality of families and difficult for them to grasp, partially because the content is presented in a highly

abstract manner. The overall "tone" to be used in this catechumenal journey should move beyond a "moralistic appeal" and should tend instead toward one that is purposeful, persuasive, encouraging, and fully oriented to emphasizing the good and beautiful aspects of married life. Completeness, precision of content, and style of accompaniment should always seek to bring to light the dignity and value of each person, as well as the dignity and value of the vocation to which they are called, with full awareness of their concrete reality. This care for presentation style is particularly important today since many engaged couples live in complex situations of cohabitation. Although these couples "glimpse" the greatness of the sacrament's mystery as compared to mere cohabitation, they often struggle to grasp the sacramental significance and the "conversion" that the choice of getting married ultimately entails. The pastoral approach should therefore be gradual, welcoming, and supportive, while also offering the witness of other Christian spouses who should welcome them and "be there for them" throughout the journey. For this reason, communities should encourage married couples to be active members in the pastoral care of married life, in their identity as spouses rather than simply as individual believers. "Personalized" experiences should be strengthened in small groups which offer space for listening and preparation — even with engaged couples separately, if necessary — so that couples are carefully guided by accompanying spouses, who can help create an atmosphere of friendship and trust. One possibility could be to meet at an accompanying couple's house to make engaged couples feel welcome and comfortable.

21. The team which will guide engaged couples during their journey may be composed of several married couples supported by a priest and other experts in family ministry, as well as religious men and women. It may be possible to include separated people who have remained faithful to the sacrament, so as to offer their constructive witness and vocational experience while showing the face of a welcoming Church which is fully rooted in reality and stands by everyone. Care should be taken to assign this ministry not to just one person, but rather to several couples, preferably of various ages, and not to assign the same team for too many years, so as to provide an appropriate turnover. Parishes and/or various pastoral groups should collaborate together in order to encourage a variety of programs and the possibility of offering everyone a chance to receive formation.

22. Several complex issues pertaining to marital sexuality or openness to life (such as responsible parenthood, artificial insemination, prenatal diagnosis, and other bioethical issues) have important ethical, relational, and spiritual repercussions on spouses which require specific formation and clarity of ideas. This is so because some ways of dealing with such issues present morally problematic aspects. Accompanying couples themselves are not always able to offer proper guidance on such issues, which are indeed extremely widespread. The involvement of people with more experience in these cases is most appropriate.[2]

23. Throughout the catechumenal method, rituals serve the function of delineating the conclusion of one phase

and the beginning of the next, and can offer couples a suitable opportunity to freely manifest their willingness to continue with the program, thus marking a gradual deepening of the journey. Moreover, rituals offer a sign of the gradual merging of faith and love of engaged couples. The following rituals could be considered ahead of the actual Rite of Marriage: entrusting couples with the Bible; presenting them to the community; blessing their engagement rings; offering them a "couple's prayer" to accompany them on their journey. These options should be considered according to the milieu of the local church. Each of these rituals may be accompanied by a retreat, which can offer opportunities for discernment about whether or not to continue to the next phase, in spiritual dialogue with members of the accompanying team. At the same time, couples could be invited to set up a "family altar" in their home during the early years of married life in order to offer a place where spouses and children can gather in prayer.

Phases and stages

24. In a long-term pastoral perspective, a pre-catechumenal phase should precede the in-depth catechumenal journey: such a phase would coincide in practice with the extended period of "remote preparation" for marriage, which begins in childhood. The actual catechumenal phase consists of three distinct stages: proximate preparation, final preparation, and accompaniment during the first years of married life. In between the pre-catechumenal phase and the actual catechumenal phase, an intermediate phase may be envisaged in which the reception of candidates takes place, which

could conclude with a ritual of entry into the marriage catechumenate. Summing up that which will be laid out in detail further on, what follows is a bullet-point list of the various phases and stages, with some rituals and retreats delineating them:

A. *Pre-catechumenal phase: remote preparation*
- Youth ministry
- Young Adult ministry

B. *Intermediate phase (lasting a few weeks): period of reception of candidates*
- Ritual of entry into the catechumenate (concluding the reception phase)

C. *Catechumenal phase*
- First stage: proximate preparation (about a year) Rite of Betrothal (concluding the proximate preparation). Brief entrance retreat into final preparation
- Second stage: final preparation (a few months). Short retreat in preparation for wedding (a few days before the celebration)
- Third stage: first years of married life (two to three years)

Two clarifications

25. Pastoral experience in large parts of the world has encountered a constant, widespread increase of demand for sacramental marriage preparation on the part of couples who are already living together, have celebrated a civil marriage, and have children. Such demand can no longer be sidestepped by the Church or flattened within programs mapped out for those who come from a minimal

journey of faith. Rather, these situations call for personalized accompaniment, or small groups, which are geared toward the maturation as a person and as a couple on the path toward Christian marriage through the rediscovery of the Faith, beginning with baptism and a gradual growth in understanding the meaning of the Rite and Sacrament of Matrimony. For such couples, local churches could consider catechumenal pathways outside the *developmental pastoral care* of young people and engaged couples — such as the one proposed in this document — which would lead to the same vocational and sacramental awareness, while taking their specific situation in life as a starting point. A new program would thus take shape in an effort to respond to the needs presented by a reality of contemporary family life which is different from that prevailing in decades past, but still eager to get closer to the Church and the "great mystery" of marriage.

26. In the following description, the pathway also presents several "rituals." Attention should be paid to how these rituals are performed and especially to how they are perceived. Although couples taking part in this type of formative approach generally react very positively, experience has also shown that there may be risks, especially in some countries, due to a culture or mentality which is particularly sensitive to rituals and their social relevance. For example, excessive public "exposure" of engaged couples — that is, with the presence of families and the entire parish community in the various rituals of the catechumenal itinerary — has sometimes led to these rituals being perceived almost as "anticipations" of marriage, engendering false expectations and undue

psychological pressure on engaged couples. Such situations could negatively influence the discernment process of engaged couples and limit their freedom, thus creating the conditions for a null celebration of marriage. Therefore, prudence and careful evaluation of how to present these rituals are recommended, according to the relevant social context. In some cases, for instance, it may be preferable for such rituals to take place only among the group of couples following the catechumenal pathway, without involving family members or others. In other cases, however, it would be better to avoid the rituals altogether.

A. Pre-catechumenal phase: remote preparation

27. Remote preparation precedes the actual catechumenal pathway. It aims, from childhood, to "prepare the ground" on which to sow the seeds of a future vocation to married life. The "ground" may be considered well-prepared if esteem for every genuine human value is instilled in children, if self-esteem and esteem for others are cultivated, if self-mastery is taught, even in small things, along with the right use of one's inclinations, respect for persons of the opposite sex, and the dignity of every human being in general.[3]

28. The Church, with considerate maternal care, shall seek the most appropriate way to "narrate" to children the plan of love that God has for each person, of which marriage is a sign, and which, even in their case, will manifest itself as a vocational call. The happiness of entire generations depends on it. After all, the vocation to family life comprises most people in the world. To this

end, a healthy Christian anthropology should be formed already in children — including the first elements of human sexuality and the theology of the body[4] — and their baptismal identity should be developed in a vocational perspective, whether to marriage or religious life.

29. The process of formation begun in children can be continued and deepened with adolescents and young people, so that they do not come to the decision to marry as if by chance and in the wake of an adolescence wounded by affective and sexual experiences which prove painful for their spiritual life. Such experiences can cause deep emotional wounds, which will spill over into adulthood in their sexual and marital lives. Faced with these wounds, the pastoral team should be able to offer the assistance of experts who can accompany these young people on a personal level. Moreover, many young people, due to a variety of reasons, including familial, social, or cultural contexts, enter adulthood without any preparation for married life, while many others have never given thought to marriage as a vocation and are therefore content to cohabitate. In most cases this occurs not because of an explicit aversion to the religious dimension, but because of ignorance of the immense richness contained in the sacramental grace of Christian marriage, or due to other social or cultural factors.[5] For this reason, pastoral workers should be formed to employ suitable language and know how to offer the Word in a way that is understandable to young people, inserted in their reality, and capable of stirring up true interest in them.

30. Young people face two dangers: the spread of a he-

donistic and consumerist mentality that robs them of every ability to understand the beautiful and profound meaning of human sexuality, on the one hand. On the other, they encounter the separation of sexuality from the lifelong commitment to marriage. Programs aimed at formation in affectivity and sexuality — within the horizon of "'a positive and prudent sex education' [offered to children] 'as they grow older'"[6] should not be limited to the horizon of love *tout court*. In the dominant cultural interpretation, love is mainly understood as romantic love; therefore, programs must be permeated by a clear marital vision of love, understood as mutual self-giving by spouses, as knowing how to love and let oneself be loved, as reciprocal exchange of affection and unconditional acceptance, and as knowing how to rejoice and suffer with each other.[7] There is a particularly urgent need to create or strengthen pastoral programs geared especially toward young people in the age of puberty and adolescence. Faced with contemporary challenges, the family cannot and is unable to act as the exclusive environment for formation in affectivity. The help of the Church is therefore required. To achieve this goal, adequate training should be provided for formators who accompany the very young in formation in sexuality and affectivity. Experts should be involved, for example, and synergy should be created with Christian-inspired counselors or pastoral projects offering affective formation, which have been approved by the diocese/eparchy or the national bishops' conference.

31. The stages of childhood, adolescence, and young adulthood form part of a single, seamless journey of

formation, which is based on two fundamental truths: "first, that man is called to live in truth and love; and second, that everyone finds fulfillment through the sincere gift of self"[8] in a vocation. Enlightening young people about the relationship which love has with truth will help them not develop a fatalistic fear regarding the mutability of feelings and the trials of time.[9]

32. The formative journey of remote preparation should receive consideration in the pastoral program of every parish or other Church community. In particular, it should be explicitly proclaimed in the context of youth ministry (including adolescent groups) and be presented as a favorable time to begin to promote the maturation of a vocation to marriage.[10] It would be appropriate to initiate collaboration with lay associations and movements to implement pastoral projects in synergy and a spirit of ecclesial communion.[11]

33. A form of accompaniment rich in closeness and witness can offer an enormous aid to young people. Young people always find it extremely interesting to listen directly to spouses tell their story as a couple, offering reasons for their "yes," or to the testimony of engaged couples — or even to those who have not yet decided to marry — who seek to live their engagement in a Christian way and as an important period of discernment and verification, including those who have made the choice to live chastely before marriage, and who tell young people about the reasons for their choice and the spiritual fruits that flow from it.[12]

34. Young people also need personalized moments, time dedicated to each individually,[13] in order to receive guidance regarding doubts and questions, to face fears and insecurities, to be assisted in reflecting on immaturity, and to learn to overcome the closure of the self while opening up to concrete love from another person.[14]

35. Many young people fail to grasp the intimate connection that exists between faith life and emotional life. Cultivating true and sincere human love prepares a person to encounter God's even greater love and facilitates the discovery (or rediscovery) of faith. At the same time, encountering God's love and discovering (or rediscovering) faith gives new meaning and depth to the experience of human love.[15] Faith possesses its own form of understanding, which flows from love and opens a person up to love.[16] Young people at this remote phase, therefore, need to be guided in harmonious growth which unites the human and spiritual dimensions of love, especially in those who approach marriage preparation with minimal experience of faith and without actively participating in the life of the Church.

36. In summary, the purposes of remote preparation are: (a) to teach children self-esteem and respect for others, and the awareness of their own dignity and respect for that of others; (b) to introduce children to Christian anthropology and the vocational perspective implicit in baptism that will lead to marriage or consecrated life; (c) to form adolescents in affectivity and sexuality in view of their future call to generous, exclusive, and faithful

love (whether in marriage, priesthood, or consecrated life); and (d) to offer young people a journey of human and spiritual growth to overcome immaturity, fears, and resistance in order to open themselves to relationships of friendship and love which are neither possessive nor narcissistic, but are rather free, generous, and self-giving.

B. Intermediate phase: reception of candidates

37. The intermediate reception phase may vary in duration: a few weeks is sufficient for those already coming from a journey of Christian formation; while a few months may be required for those who, in addition to making an initial discernment regarding their engagement, need to deepen their baptismal identity. A welcoming phase may also be provided for couples who join later in the program.

38. The reception period should not be limited to a hasty meeting to present the couples and deal with bureaucratic formalities. Rather, it should be prepared as a personalized period of encounter and getting to know each other. A determining factor for success will be established by how the pastoral team creates a welcoming and friendly environment. This factor applies both to those who come from a period of remote formation — and thus enjoy an established faith life and ecclesial participation — and to those who are approaching the parish community for the first time.[17] In the latter case, especially when working with people far from religious practice or even with near ignorance of faith, the period of reception should become a proclamation of the

kerygma, so that the merciful love of Christ may create an authentic "spiritual place" in which couples are welcomed.[18]

39. Not only does the "first proclamation" of the faith have a kerygmatic character, but the Church should treat the Sacrament of Matrimony itself as an opportunity for genuine proclamation, especially for people who lack a mature experience of faith and ecclesial involvement. They must be able to see in married couples, and experience for themselves, that married life is the answer to the deepest expectations of the human person in their desire for reciprocity, communion, and fruitfulness, both physical and spiritual.[19] The catechetical program shall therefore seek to bring out the conjugal and familial nature of love, while highlighting each of its special characteristics: totality, complementarity, uniqueness, finality, fidelity, fruitfulness, and public nature. The "Gospel proclamation" on marriage should show that these characteristics flow from the intrinsic dynamism of human love. In other words, fidelity, uniqueness, finality, and totality form the "essential dimensions" of every authentic bond of love which is understood, desired, and consistently lived out by a man and a woman; they are not just the "well-known characteristics" of "Catholic" marriage. Consequently, the Sacrament of Matrimony may be presented to couples not as a mere moral or legal obligation to endure, but rather as a gift, an offer of grace, and an aid which God offers them precisely to fulfill the demands of authentic love. In the final analysis, pastoral care of marriage should always employ a joyful and kerygmatic tone — vigorous

and at the same time purposeful — in line with what Pope John Paul II and Pope Francis have suggested.[20] The witness, beauty, and driving force of Christian families may come to the aid of pastors in the face of these challenges.[21]

40. During this period of getting to know the couples to be invited to the marriage catechumenate, special attention should be paid to those who have chosen to cohabitate without marrying, but who nevertheless remain open to the religious dimension and are willing to approach the Church. These couples should be warmly welcomed without legalism but rather with an understanding gaze.[22] Appreciation should be expressed for their "desire for family," while avoiding putting any pressure on them, but simply inviting them to participate in a period of listening and reflection. It should be made clear to them that the final decision whether to celebrate sacramental marriage will be made by them — autonomously and out of personal conviction — as the fruit of this discernment period.[23]

41. The reception period may be conducted by a married couple, joined by a priest, whenever possible. The program may consist of a few meetings held in a comfortable, friendly atmosphere, in order to get to know the couple and understand their true motives for asking to prepare for marriage, as well as to embark on a journey of discernment. This provides an opportune time to purify any ambiguous motives which may lie behind the request to marry in the Church. If the couple has drifted away from religious practice, it is a good time

to offer them an initial proclamation of the Faith. Time should be allowed for the couple to reason together, consider their decision, and make an informed choice. Therefore, conversations with the candidates should take place over the space of several meetings. In order to direct and provide concreteness to the couple's work of introspection, a written outline of their reflection may be produced in view of subsequent meetings.

42. Both for those who already embrace the religious and ecclesial dimensions, and for those who lack an experience of faith, it is important that candidates manifest an inner readiness to embark upon a journey of faith conversion as part of the marriage catechumenate. Only when couples have allowed their decision to mature shall they move on to the next stage.

43. As previously mentioned, the fact that large numbers of baptized people who ask to marry in the Church do so without a mature experience of faith and ecclesial involvement calls for a pastoral attitude which offers them greater attention than has so far been afforded.[24] Every care must be taken to embrace these situations with the correct attitude. Superficial and hasty solutions should be avoided, and ministers should instead view these cases as precious opportunities for proclamation and closeness to our brothers and sisters who are "young in the faith." These couples must be accompanied toward the fullness of Christian life and toward the fullness of the Sacrament of Matrimony,[25] so that "every man and every woman who marry celebrate the sacrament of marriage not only validly but also fruitfully."[26]

44. Nonpracticing baptized persons with little or no experience of faith must necessarily receive an explicit invitation to embark upon the catechumenal journey, with the aim of accepting the kerygma, forming their mind and heart according to the teachings of Jesus, and inserting them into the life of the Church. Indeed, the Magisterium of the last three popes has reaffirmed the relationship between faith and the Sacrament of Matrimony.[27] The presence of a living and explicit faith in couples is obviously the ideal situation to achieve the goal of arriving at the wedding with a clear and conscious intention to celebrate a true marriage: one which is indissoluble and exclusive, directed toward the good of the spouses, and open to children. Nonetheless, there remains a necessary condition for access to the Sacrament of Matrimony and its validity: The condition is not a certain a priori "minimum level of faith" on the part of the betrothed,[28] but rather consists in their intention to do what the Church intends to accomplish in the celebration of marriage between baptized persons.[29]

45. On a pastoral level, the various situations of baptized persons who manifest an insufficient disposition to believe should be carefully evaluated.

In cases where the engaged couple explicitly and formally rejects that which the Church intends to accomplish in the celebration of marriage, they cannot be admitted to the sacramental celebration.[30] It sometimes happens that this refusal is truly present in the minds and hearts of the engaged without their being fully aware of it, or without their openly manifesting it. Therefore, pastoral workers have the grave duty to bring out the true intentions of the engaged persons, so that they might themselves become aware of their intentions and manifest them sincerely to those who accompany them, in order to prevent the preparation and celebration of marriage from being reduced to purely external acts.

If, on the other hand, the bride and groom possess an imperfect disposition without refuting what the Church intends to accomplish, then their admission to the celebration of the sacrament should not be ruled out. Pastoral agents should not fail to take advantage of this situation as a favorable moment for couples to rediscover their faith and bring it to greater maturity. This can be done by helping them return to the roots of their baptism, reviving the "seed" of divine life that has already been sown in them, and inviting them to reflect on their choice for sacramental marriage as a consolidation, sanctification, and fulfillment of their love.[31] Only by rediscovering the gift of being Christians — new creatures, children of God, and loved and called by him — can clear-headed discernment about the Sacrament of Matrimony be possible, in continuity with one's baptismal identity and as the fulfillment of a unique call from God. Indeed, the awakening of faith naturally leads a person to perceive the power of the sacramental grace present in marriage and to dispose oneself to receive it in the best way possible.[32]

46. Some situations — increasingly common in every region of the world — deserve special attention and pastoral care: These include couples in which one person is

Christian and the other belongs to a non-Christian religion, or in which one person is Catholic while the other confesses a different Christian denomination which is not Catholic. At the same time, both members of a couple may be Catholic, but one of them may refuse to follow the catechumenal journey. In all such cases, the parish priest shall have the responsibility to assess the best way forward for marriage preparation.

47. At the end of the reception phase, when the decision to enter the catechumenal journey has matured, the couple may enter the first stage of formation for marriage (proximate preparation). This passage can be expressed with a rite of entry into the actual catechumenate. The ritual should employ a simple format so as to avoid making it seem in any way to be a "marriage rite," and may include the presentation of the couples to the community during the Sunday celebration, with a short introduction, a prayer suitable for the purpose, and a concrete gesture — for example, the handing over of the Bible. It should be made clear to the community that the couples are entering into the catechumenal journey as a period of discernment regarding their choice to marry. Alternatively, especially if cultural reasons mean it would be more appropriate to avoid a "public" and community ritual, couples may be invited to a more intimate moment of prayer, which could take place among the group of new catechumens, together with the accompanying team, and include the handing over of the Bible or some other symbol suitable for the occasion.

C. Catechumenal phase

48. The catechumenate shall consist of a more or less lengthy period of formation which includes proximate preparation, final preparation, and accompaniment during the first years of marriage. The following indications are intended as mere guidelines and should be implemented with pastoral intelligence according to the concrete possibilities of each particular church.

Proximate preparation, in general, should ideally last approximately one year, depending on the couple's previous experience of faith and ecclesial involvement. Having confirmed their decision to marry — a moment which could be sealed by a betrothal ritual — couples may then begin the final preparation for marriage, lasting a few months, which should be set up as an actual initiation into the Sacrament of Matrimony. The duration of these stages should be adapted — repeating what has already been stated — according to the religious, cultural, and social aspects of the local environment, as well as the personal situation of each couple. One essential element to safeguard is the regularity of encounters, so as to accustom couples to responsibly care for their vocation and marriage.

First stage: proximate preparation

49. The marriage catechumenate in this initial stage shall assume the character of a true journey of faith, during which the Christian message should be rediscovered and revisited in its perennial newness and freshness.[33] Together with the revival of a catechesis of Christian initiation into the faith, the sacraments of

Christian initiation — baptism, confirmation, and the Eucharist — should be revisited, along with the Sacrament of Reconciliation. Sacred Scripture — especially Genesis, the prophets, and the Song of Songs — should provide a constant point of reference for couples, since they contain foundational texts and symbolism for the Sacrament of Matrimony. Additionally, candidates for marriage should be gradually introduced to Christian prayer — individual, communal, and as a couple — in order to acquire a habit of prayer which will offer immense support for their future married life, especially in difficult moments.[34] Preparation for the unique mission of the spouses should not be neglected at this stage, since marriage is a sacrament geared toward mission.[35]

50. Couples shall be helped to approach the life of the Church and take part in it.[36] They may be gently and warmly invited to participate in moments of prayer, such as the Sunday Eucharist, confession, and retreats, as well as moments of celebration and community. The invitation should be made gradually (according to each couple's concrete experience), so that they might feel at ease in the various spheres of community life — liturgical, charitable, and festive — without coercion. Couples should be helped to feel like recipients of an "undeserved, unconditional, and gratuitous"[37] mercy, for having received the call and gift of being part of the great family of Christ's disciples.

51. Besides revisiting the Christian initiation into the Faith, proximate preparation shall also provide an initiation into the Sacrament of Matrimony. For this rea-

son, a journey of reflection on the positive aspects of marriage must be carried out at this stage, so that newer generations of spouses shall arrive at the sacrament with greater awareness. They will be more aware because they understand the essential aspects that make it a sacrament and recognize the graces that flow from it and the good things it promises, and are thus able to prepare themselves to welcome those graces and embrace those benefits as a gift.[38]

52. An important element of this stage shall be to deepen understanding about everything related to the relationship of couples and the interpersonal dynamics it entails, including the "rules" of relationship, its laws of growth, and the elements that strengthen relationship and those that weaken it. Couples can draw great benefit from learning more about the various psychological and affective attitudes typical of men and women, their differing sensitivities, their different ways of establishing and nurturing relationships, and the characteristic "nuances" of male and female souls which come into play in every relationship between two people.[39] Couples should come to know and understand the anthropological reality of the human person in general, and of the two sexes in particular, created and willed by God, since this aspect constitutes the "human material" forming the basis of the marital relationship. There exists a "truth" of the human person, as well as a unique "truth" regarding man and woman, which must be accepted and embraced, because anything that goes against these "truths" or tramples on them, even within marriage, generates discomfort and suffering.[40]

53. There are many other aspects related to the human reality of the person and the couple which need to be properly explored: the human dynamics of conjugal sexuality, the proper understanding of responsible paternity and maternity, and the raising of children. Catechesis and Christian teachings will help consolidate knowledge of the truth related to marriage and the formation of personal conscience.[41] At this stage, the experience of spouses with several years of marriage behind them can offer a precious contribution.

54. As engaged couples deepen their understanding of the human reality of the person and the couple, they also need to become aware of personal psychological and/or affective shortcomings, which can weaken or even completely nullify the commitment of self-giving and mutual love which spouses promise each other. However, the discovery of eventual personal shortcomings must not necessarily result in the abandonment of the choice to embrace married life. It can also become a stimulus to begin a more serious process of growth to prepare the person to arrive at a condition of sufficient inner freedom and psychological maturity to embrace married life with joy and serenity.[42]

55. The specific goal of this stage is to finalize each couple's discernment about their vocation to marriage. This may lead to the free, responsible, and deliberated decision to enter into marriage, or it may lead to the equally free and deliberated decision to end the relationship and not to marry. In order to offer "material" to assist the couple's discernment, this stage shall explore the

theology of marriage, as well as the many other aspects related to the "practical aspects" of married life. These aspects include: a person's intentions regarding their willingness to make a lifelong commitment and regarding children; potential incompatibilities; and the expectations and personal opinion each person holds regarding love and married life. The goal is to help couples understand the difference between the *"preparation of a wedding"* and *"preparation to a marriage."*

The future spouses shall be invited to discern realistically and sincerely — each on their own behalf and together — whether the marriage corresponds to what they desire and that to which the Lord is calling them.[43] Such discernment, which shall be conducted within the framework of dialogue on the spiritual, personal, and couple levels, should not be underestimated, since the experience of the ecclesiastical tribunals shows the extreme fragility of couples who, despite their initial faith and enthusiasm, lack the basic requirements which would have been necessary to contract marriage: capacity and will.[44]

56. Every individual shall be accompanied on their journey of reflection, conversion, and understanding of the meaning of married life within a mindset of respect, patience, and mercy.[45] However, a mercy-filled perspective never leads to obscuring "the Gospel demands of truth and charity proclaimed by the Church."[46] At the same time, the Church must never fail to proclaim the divine plan for human love and marriage in all its beauty and grandeur.[47] The highest and noblest ideals may

seem demanding and arduous, but they are also those that most powerfully attract the human soul, stimulate it to surpass itself, and confer value and dignity on our earthly existence.

57. In this regard, the Church must never lack the courage to proclaim the precious virtue of chastity,[48] no matter how directly it contrasts with the prevailing mentality. Chastity should be presented as an authentic "ally of love," not as its negation. Chastity, indeed, is the privileged path to learn to respect the individuality and dignity of others, without subordinating them to one's own desires. Chastity teaches engaged couples the times and ways of true, gentle, and generous love, and prepares them for the authentic gift of self to be lived out during a lifetime of marriage.[49] The virtue of chastity, therefore, should be explained in both its negative dimension, which requires each person to abstain from a disordered use of sexuality according to their state of life, as well as in its highly important positive dimension which entails freedom from the possession of another person — in physical, moral, and spiritual terms. This freedom, in the case of the call to marriage, is of fundamental importance in guiding and nourishing conjugal love, preserving it from any form of manipulation. Chastity ultimately teaches a person to be faithful to the truth of their love, in every state of life. For engaged couples, this means living chastity in continence and once married living conjugal intimacy with moral rectitude.[50]

Chastity lived in continence allows a relationship to mature gradually and thoroughly. Indeed, when, as often occurs, the sexual-genital dimension becomes the primary, if not exclusive, element holding a couple together, all other aspects inevitably fall into the background or are obscured, impeding the relationship from progressing. On the contrary, chastity lived in continence enables the engaged couple to get to know one another better. This is so because it prevents the relationship from becoming focused on the physical use of the other person, while also fostering deeper dialogue, more complete openness of the heart, and the emergence of all aspects of the personality — human, spiritual, intellectual, and emotional — so as to allow for true growth in relationship, personal communion, and the discovery of the other's richness and limitations. Therein lies the true purpose of the period of engagement.[51]

Even when addressing cohabiting couples, it is never useless to speak about the virtue of chastity. This virtue teaches every baptized person, in every condition of life, the correct use of sexuality, and for this reason, even in married life, chastity is extremely useful. As spouses, the importance of the values and awareness taught by the virtue of chastity emerges even more clearly: respect for other people; concern never to subject another to personal desires; patience and gentleness with one's spouse in times of physical or spiritual difficulty; and fortitude and self-dominance, which are required in moments of absence or illness, etc.[52] In this context, the lived experience of Christian spouses can be useful to help explain the importance of the virtue of chastity within marriage and the family.

58. Special attention should be paid to the spiritual method employed during the stage of proximate preparation. During this period of formation and initiation, the transmission of theoretical content should necessarily be accompanied by the invitation to a spiritual journey, which includes experiences of prayer (personal, communal, and as a couple), celebration of the sacraments, spiritual retreats, moments of Eucharistic Adoration, missionary experiences, and charitable activities (depending on the pastoral context).

59. At the conclusion of this stage, the Rite of Betrothal could take place as a sign of entry into the subsequent stage of final preparation. This rite — which includes the blessing of the betrothed and their engagement rings (in places where this custom is commonplace) — expresses its full meaning only when celebrated and lived in faith, since the rite offers the opportunity for the couple to ask the Lord for the graces needed to grow in love and to prepare worthily for the Sacrament of Matrimony.[53] The most appropriate moment for the celebration of this rite shall be chosen in dialogue with the members of the accompanying team and the ordained minister.

60. Given its personal and ecclesial value, the Rite of Betrothal should certainly be reevaluated as a significant moment in the journey of faith toward the Sacrament of Matrimony. In this rite, the Church "entrusts" couples with the mission of engagement, which consists in discernment. By ritualizing this moment, couples grow in awareness that they are called in the months ahead to reach an inner certainty regarding the decision to

marry and regarding the person whom they will marry. Each person must embrace prudent human judgment and the light of faith to formulate in their own heart the following conclusion about their future spouse: "This person is the companion with whom I choose to live in a relationship of authentic, faithful, and lasting love and with whom I want to build a family; this is the person whom the Lord has given me to walk a path of holiness together, and who will be father/mother of the children God will give us, and with whom I will live our 'mission' of marriage for a lifetime." The goal and "mission" of discernment is to arrive at this certainty, and is the responsibility which the Church entrusts to the couple, inviting them to accept it with due seriousness.

61. The Rite of Betrothal is sometimes understood as a "promise of marriage."[54] However, no legal obligation to contract marriage derives from this promise, and the freedom of the contracting party to express matrimonial consent is always safeguarded. Moreover, the celebration of the rite should in no way be confused with marriage. For this reason, neither the promise of marriage nor the special blessing of the engaged couple should ever be performed during the celebration of Mass.[55] The outline of the celebration should be simple and sober: opening rites, proclamation of the Word of God, prayers of the faithful, perhaps a "sign of commitment" — for example, exchange of engagement rings — prayer of blessing, and conclusion of the rite. The vocational aspect of marriage should be explicitly recalled, and the Scripture readings and prayers for couples should be focused on married love, which is purified, strengthened,

and made stable and generous by the very love of God poured into human hearts.

62. The fact that the "status" of engaged couples is somehow formalized at this stage in the pathway is of considerable importance, and this status should be understood in its social and ecclesial relevance. For couples who cohabitate, as an example, the new status can help provide an "objective" aspect to their relationship — perhaps previously only understood by some cohabitating couples as personal and "private" — by endowing it with a public character, thereby making the couple feel part of a welcoming community that accompanies them and cares about their union. This stage also serves as an invitation for all engaged couples to understand that their future status as "spouses," for which they are preparing, greatly exceeds their affective relationship, confined to the private sphere of emotional experiences, and will engender a new reality — a family, whose social and ecclesial role is of fundamental importance.[56]

63. To summarize, the aims of proximate preparation are: (a) to revisit a catechesis of initiation into the Christian Faith and to draw couples into the life of the Church; (b) to begin a unique initiation into the Sacrament of Matrimony and to come to a clear awareness of its essential aspects; (c) to deepen understanding of the facets of the couple's relationship and to become aware of psychological and affective shortcomings; (d) to complete an initial phase of discernment about the couple's vocation to marriage; (e) to continue more decisively along a spiritual journey.[57]

Second stage: final preparation

64. The final preparation for the marriage takes place in the months leading up to the wedding celebration.[58] The start of this new stage may be marked by a brief spiritual retreat and the handing over of a symbolic object, such as a prayer that couples recite together when they meet.

65. The main content of the journey of preparation undertaken thus far should be recalled. Emphasis needs to be placed on the indispensable conditions of freedom (within the couple and as a couple) and full awareness regarding the commitments assumed in the choice to be made. Those commitments are linked to the essential characteristics of marriage (indissolubility, unity, fidelity, fecundity) and will form the specific content of the interviews with the pastor required by canon law.[59] At the same time, the doctrinal, moral, and spiritual aspects of marriage should be recalled. In this way, an opportunity will arise to profitably return to the essential points of the initiation into the Sacrament of Matrimony already carried out in the previous stage of proximate preparation. On the other hand, this content may also be presented as a true "proclamation of the Gospel of marriage" for couples who have not participated in that previous stage.[60] Various circumstances may arise whereby some couples enter the catechumenal journey at this stage, which means that the final preparation offers them the only concrete possibility of receiving a minimum of formation in view of the celebration of the Sacrament of Matrimony. It would be appropriate to involve these couples in additional personalized conversations with the pastoral team for marriage prepa-

ration in order to offer them the proper care and attention; to explore together more personal aspects of their choice to marry, depending on the couple's situation (they may have children or may have cohabitated for a long time); and to create a relationship of trust, cordiality, and friendship with the couples of the accompaniment team. At the same time, these "new" couples — who have not participated in the proximate preparation stage — should also participate in the group meetings so that they feel welcomed and included in the ecclesial reality in a relatively short time.

66. Spiritual experiences shall be offered which are specifically designed for couples (listening to the Word, celebration of the sacraments, moments of personal and community prayer) in order to constantly return to the encounter with the Lord as the source and center of all Christian life. Indeed, the catechumenal approach should always rise above a mere sociological view of marriage so as to help spouses understand the mystery of grace involved in the sacrament and, more generally, to aid in grasping the spiritual dynamic of Christian life that forms the basis of marriage.

67. For this reason, it would be useful to reformulate the kerygmatic proclamation of Christ's redemption that saves us from the reality of sin, which always looms over human life. Spouses must never forget that sin is ultimately the real threat to their love.[61] Estrangement from God is far more serious than any psychological shortcoming or imperfect interpersonal dynamic, since distance from God triggers a spiral of closure and self-

ishness in the human heart that hinders true love, because it prevents openness, respect, and generosity toward another person. Therefore, in order to be able to grow daily in mutual love, sin, which "lies in wait" at the door of the heart (see Gn 4:7), must be mastered with the help of grace. Moreover, couples should have recourse to God's forgiveness in the Sacrament of Reconciliation, through which God bestows his love, which is more powerful than any sin.[62]

68. As they approach the wedding, couples should become aware that they are not spectators but rather, in the name of Christ, ministers of the celebration of their marriage. For this reason, ample space shall be devoted to the liturgical preparation of couples, so as to help them fully understand the signs and meaning of the Rite of Marriage.[63] The liturgical Rite of Marriage contains a pedagogical approach, which encompasses the richness of anthropology (the life of people), Scripture (God's plan for the family), the Church (the mission of the family in the Church and in the world), and spirituality (the journey of conversion and response to the action of the Spirit), such that it constitutes the outline for this stage. Couples should be taught that their married life will take on an extraordinary value as a "sacramental sign": in the marriage rite they become a permanent sacrament of Christ who loves the Church. Just as ordained ministers are called to become "living icons" of Christ the priest, so are Christian spouses called to become "living icons" of Christ the bridegroom. Beyond any words, the very way spouses live and relate to one another should manifest to the world the generous

and total love with which Christ loves the Church and all humanity.[64] Indeed, such is the extraordinary witness which so many Christian spouses offer the world: Their capacity for dedication to each other and to their children, as well as their capacity for fidelity, patience, forgiveness, and compassion, are such that others can sense a "supernatural source" underlying their relationship, something "beyond" which is not humanly explicable, but which unceasingly nourishes their love to the point of making it appear almost heroic.[65]

69. In view of the wedding celebration, care shall be taken to involve the spouses in the choice of readings for the Mass, and possibly even the options provided for other parts of the rite — for example, the various aspects of the entrance rite, the moment of the marriage blessing, the formularies of the prayers of the faithful, the hymns, etc. One aspect which should be heavily emphasized is the awareness of a new outpouring of the Holy Spirit during the Rite of Marriage. This effusion of the Spirit forms part of the dynamism of grace initiated in baptism, but also provides a new aspect to the divine charity infused in us from baptism, one which now takes on the features of "conjugal charity." This new bestowal of the Spirit renews the hearts of spouses and directs their conjugal love toward, and transforms it into, a love which contains the depth and inexhaustible power of divine love — that is, precisely, "conjugal charity."[66] Those saints invoked in the litanies also act as intercessors in view of this outpouring. Couples can derive great benefit by invoking the saints or blessed spouses of our times, who have already lived the experience of being husbands and wives, fathers and

mothers. They could also invoke other holy intercessors who are important for the spouses so as to enhance the dignity of married life within the Church community and help everyone understand the beauty and strength of this sacrament in the economy of salvation.

70. A one- or two-day spiritual retreat would offer great benefit if held a few days before the wedding. Although this may seem unrealistic given the many commitments related to wedding planning, nevertheless great benefits have been produced when it has been implemented. Indeed, it is precisely the hustle and bustle of the many practical tasks associated with the upcoming celebration that can distract the betrothed from what matters most: the celebration of the sacrament and the encounter with the Lord who comes to "inhabit" their human love by filling it with his divine love. Excessive anxiety about "things to do" can cause distraction and risks overshadowing all the spiritual preparation which has filled the previous months. In this sense, a short retreat in the run-up to the wedding can help refocus on the essentials and turn the couple's gaze away from secondary things and instead toward the Lord, who comes to meet the bride and groom and brings to fulfillment the vocation to which he has called them. In those cases where an actual retreat is impossible, even a shorter time of prayer (such as an evening meeting, or "prayer vigil") could serve this purpose. In any case, the invitation to such a retreat should take account of a couple's concrete life commitments, as well as the effective possibility they have to make time for a retreat before the wedding celebration, so as not to make it unworkable.

71. Shortly before the wedding, couples should celebrate the Sacrament of Reconciliation, either during the aforementioned spiritual retreat or at a "prayer vigil," or even in another context.[67] Experience shows that receiving God's forgiveness — perhaps even making a more involved confession covering previously confessed sins, if appropriate — prepares spouses better than anything else to welcome the grace which God offers them in the Sacrament of Matrimony, since it removes feelings of profound guilt resulting from past "baggage," grants inner peace, and directs the spirit toward God's grace and mercy and toward that which really matters. It also diverts attention away from the merely material aspects of the wedding. Moreover, confession ahead of marriage — which sometimes occurs after years of "avoiding" the Sacrament of Reconciliation — offers many people a chance to return to the regular reception of the sacraments. A communal celebration of the Sacrament of Reconciliation may also be considered wherever possible. Such a celebration may involve the participation of the engaged couple's respective families, along with the marriage witnesses and others wishing to participate, so that the gift of divine mercy might be poured out on their families, which also require internal reconciliation and need to be strengthened in communion. In this way, all who participate in the wedding may be helped to live this moment in the correct frame of mind.

72. The involvement of parents, witnesses, and close family members in a time of prayer before the wedding, even outside the celebration of confession, can offer a meaningful occasion for everyone to gather around the

new couple and for the bride and groom to receive their parents' blessing, as is traditional in the Bible (see Tb 10:11–13; 11:17). It also allows relatives and friends to understand that they represent and manifest the ecclesial community, which welcomes the new family within the larger Church family that feels duty bound to support the newlyweds.

73. To summarize, the aims of the final preparation stage are: (a) to recall the doctrinal, moral, and spiritual aspects of marriage (also explicitly discussing the contents of the prescribed canonical interviews); (b) to have spiritual experiences of encounter with the Lord; (c) to prepare for a conscious and fruitful participation in the liturgy of matrimony.[68]

Third stage: accompaniment during first years of married life

74. The catechumenal pathway does not conclude with the celebration of marriage. In fact, the entire process should not be understood as an isolated act, but rather as the entry into a "permanent state," which therefore requires a unique "ongoing formation" involving reflection, dialogue, and help from the Church.[69] For this reason, the first years of married life need to be "accompanied,"[70] and newlyweds should not be left in solitude.[71]

75. Newlyweds should be made aware that the celebration of marriage is the beginning of a journey, and that the couple still constitutes an "open project," not a "completed work."[72] Therefore, newlyweds need to receive assistance during this very early stage, as they

begin to gain experience of the "project of life," which is inscribed in marriage but not yet fully realized. Indeed, the grace contained in the sacrament is not automatically actuated, but rather requires the spouses to cooperate with it by responsibly taking on the tasks and challenges that married life presents.[73]

76. In order to accomplish all this, couples shall be offered the opportunity to continue the catechumenal journey through periodic meetings — possibly monthly or with some other frequency according to the discretion of the accompanying team and the availability of the couples — as well as other encounters, both in community and as a couple.[74] If the married couple changes residence and parish, it would be good to integrate them into the new parish by inviting them to attend the accompaniment program along with other spouses of their new community.

77. This is an opportune time to offer a true "marriage mystagogy." The term *mystagogy* means an "introduction to the mystery"; in other words, it is a particular type of catechesis dating back to the early centuries of Christianity which the pastors of the Church addressed to the newly baptized in order to help them understand the mystery that took place in the baptism they had received at the solemn Easter Vigil.[75] Mystagogical catechesis was often punctuated by rhetorical questions, such as "Do you know what you have received?" and "Do you know what the Lord has done in you?" This form of catechesis following the celebration of baptism was intended to help the initiated gradually deepen

their understanding of the sacrament, first regarding its ritual and symbolic meaning — by explaining the spiritual content of each aspect of the rite — but also in relation to its moral and existential implications. The newly baptized were thus enlightened about the concrete life implications of what had been celebrated.

This style of mystagogical catechesis can be applied to marriage. By returning to the various moments of the marriage rite, its rich symbolic and spiritual meaning can be explored in depth, along with its concrete consequences in married life. These aspects include: exchange of consent (the desire to be united, rather than a passing sentiment, which forms the basis of marriage: a will which is always in need of strengthening);[76] blessing of the signs that evoke marriage — for example, the rings (the promise of fidelity always requiring renewal);[77] solemn blessing of the bride and groom (the grace of God descending on the human relationship, enveloping and sanctifying it, a grace requiring constant openness);[78] and remembrance of the spouses in the heart of the Eucharistic prayer (conjugal love constantly immersed in Christ's paschal mystery invigorating it and deepening it).[79] Ultimately, mystagogical marriage catechesis, like baptismal catechesis, addresses the following invitation to the couple: "Become what you are! You are now spouses; therefore, live more and more as spouses! The Lord has blessed and 'filled' your union with grace, so put that grace to good use!" To accomplish this, spouses should be helped to feel the presence of Christ in the Sacrament of Matrimony itself, not only in the other sacraments. Christ is present in their midst as spouses: He nourishes their relationship daily, and they can turn to him together in prayer. The grace of the sacrament is at work in them and is manifested in their daily lives. Spouses, therefore, must be helped to discern the "signs" of Christ's presence in their union.[80]

It frequently happens that young spouses focus much attention on the need to earn money and raise children, so they cease seeking to improve the quality of their relationship and forget the presence of God in their love. Young spouses should be helped to learn how to find time to deepen their friendship and welcome God's grace. Premarital chastity certainly favors this journey, because it offers time for the newlyweds to be together and get to know each other better, without immediately worrying about procreation and childrearing.

78. From the very beginning of married life, the couple needs to receive concrete assistance to live their interpersonal relationship in all serenity. There are many new things to be learned: accepting the other person's differences, which are immediately manifested;[81] overcoming unrealistic expectations about living as a couple and learning to consider marriage a journey of growth;[82] managing conflicts that inevitably arise;[83] knowing the various stages through which every relationship of love passes;[84] conversing frankly to strike a balance between personal needs and those of the couple and the family;[85] acquiring daily habits that are healthy;[86] delineating a correct relationship with each spouse's family of origin from the very beginning;[87] laying the groundwork for a shared spirituality as a couple;[88] and much more.

Among the various possible proposals, spouses could be urged to keep a "Marriage Diary" in which to note joys and sufferings and everything that constitutes the concrete experience of their lives, as a sort of periodic verification of marital communion. The diary would be a type of "holy writing" to consign to memory every significant moment touched by the grace of the Holy Spirit; it could become a means to transmit the faith within the family: a "memorial" of the grace of the Holy Spirit working in the family.

79. Numerous aspects of married and family life may become topics of dialogue and catechesis during these initial years. It is essential, for example, to enlighten couples on the delicate topic of sexuality within marriage,[89] along with related issues — that is, the transmission of life and regulation of births, as well as other issues regarding morality and bioethics.[90] Another area which should not be overlooked relates to the raising of children, in both the human and Christian spheres, which constitutes a serious responsibility of parents. Couples should be made aware and adequately formed in this area, given the increasingly widespread tendency to be divided on the issue or not to deal with the task of educating and raising children by delegating it to others.[91] The Church's teaching on this theme offers spouses a treasure trove of wisdom which, when presented properly, is greatly appreciated and welcomed by spouses.

80. This stage of the catechumenate is therefore one of "apprenticeship," during which the closeness and concrete suggestions of more experienced married couples

may offer great guidance as they share with younger couples what they have learned "along the way."[92]

Grandparents' willingness to care for grandchildren is also a great resource. This allows spouses to take time to be together. At times, however, such assistance is not forthcoming, forcing the spouses to seek alternative solutions. However, such examples of generosity and help for young spouses are wonderful signs of charity.

81. Marriage ministry must be centered on the marriage bond.[93] Couples should be assisted whenever they face new difficulties and helped to seek above all to defend and consolidate their marriage union, for their own good and for the good of their children. Post-marriage meetings should necessarily insist on the sacredness of the marital bond and, as experience shows, on the fact that the goods — spiritual, psychological, and material — that result from the preservation of the union are always far superior to those that one hopes to obtain from an eventual separation. Such an approach will help teach the proper patience, fortitude, and prudence to have in times of difficulty, learning not to see the dissolution of the marital bond as a hasty solution to problems, as couples are unfortunately often advised.

By learning to overcome hard times, spouses mature in love and the union emerges fortified: Every crisis presents a moment for growth and an opportunity to make a "quantum leap" in the relationship, which is called to deepen and grow more authentic.[94] Just as in the Christian life one "trains" in the "combat of faith" (1 Tm

6:12), so in married life spouses must train to "defend" their marriage from all the inner and outer, human and spiritual, social and cultural threats which can undermine its solidity and very existence. Couples should be offered assistance in the form of spiritual accompaniment, practical solutions, and strategies derived from experience and psychological guidance. It will also be useful to point couples to places and people — counseling centers or families who make themselves available — to whom they can turn for help if difficulties arise.

82. The couple's journey must be focused on the encounter with Christ: The couple needs to continually turn to Christ and be nourished by his presence. In particular, newlyweds must perceive the extraordinary opportunity offered to them in the Sacrament of the Eucharist and the Sacrament of Reconciliation, which create a living connection with Jesus and an opportunity to be conformed to him.[95] The Eucharist offers spouses the grace to overcome their own closures and selfishness.[96] The Sacrament of Reconciliation offers spouses the infinite richness of God's mercy, who in his Son always forgives us. In this way, they learn to be patient and merciful with each other, because forgiveness received becomes forgiveness given, according to Jesus' teaching: "Should not you have had mercy on your fellow servant, as I had mercy on you?" (Mt 18:33).[97] Therefore, the encounter with Christ in the sacraments gradually helps the unique *marital identity* of Christian spouses to mature.

83. The Church's constant and permanent care for spouses can be manifested through various pastoral means:[98]

listening to the Word of God, especially through *lectio divina*; meetings to reflect on issues relevant to marital and family life; involvement of couples in liturgical celebrations especially designed for them; periodic spiritual retreats for spouses; Eucharistic Adoration organized with meditations taken from the biographies of saintly spouses; spiritual conversations and accompaniment; participation in family groups to promote conversations with other families; and involvement in charitable and missionary activities.[99] Spouses need to develop a true "marital spirituality" which nurtures and sustains the unique path to holiness that they travel in married life.[100]

The wedding anniversary should be celebrated as part of a community liturgical celebration, along with a special blessing for the spouses. On major anniversaries — for example, every five years — a renewal of marriage vows could be suggested to the bride and groom. These pastoral tools and others can help families feel that they are an integral part of their Church community, since it celebrates with them and shares their joys and journey, thus becoming a "family of families."[101]

84. As couples develop their marital identity, their sense of mission, which flows from the sacrament,[102] should grow. Therefore, as the catechumenal pathway for married life draws to an end at this time, couples need to be invited to become part of the ordinary family ministry in their parish or the Church community with which they have established some connection. Newlyweds, for example, may be gradually invited to participate in the catechumenal preparation for marriage of new

groups of engaged couples, as well as in community life and youth ministry, taking on special roles in community organization. Groups could be formed to reflect on marital spirituality (even possibly with the assistance of family movements) and marriage ministry.

85. To summarize, the aims of accompaniment in the early years of married life are: (a) to present a "mystagogical marriage catechesis" exploring the spiritual and existential implications of the Sacrament of Matrimony; (b) to help married couples embark upon a healthy path in their interpersonal relationship from the outset; (c) to explore in depth the themes of sexuality in married life, the transmission of life, and the raising of children; (d) to instill in couples the firm will to defend their marriage bond in any crisis situation that may arise; (e) to facilitate an encounter with Christ to provide an indispensable source of renewal of the grace of marriage and to foster a marital spirituality; and (f) to recall the meaning of the unique mission of Christian spouses.

86. As a corollary to this proposal, there prevails an urgency to provide more adequate formation for priests, seminarians, and lay people (including married couples) regarding the ministry of accompanying young people toward marriage. Priests/religious and pastoral workers should receive ongoing, systematic formation in view of the marriage catechumenate, in order to overcome old habits and to be formed in a style of accompaniment and understanding of the content (theological, moral, bioethical, and spiritual) which is relevant for modern-day couples, who often already cohabitate and are rais-

ing children when they approach the Church with the desire to marry. In many pastoral contexts, the proper formation of seminarians and priests is proving indispensable, one more centered on the contemporary challenges of marriage and family ministry, including issues related to morality in the sexual, marital, and bioethical spheres, which are now part of the daily life of families in many parts of the world. Therefore, for the purposes of an efficacious and effective participation of spouses as pastoral ministers, it is essential to understand the bond of complementarity and ecclesial co-responsibility that exists between the *ordo sacerdotalis* and *ordo coniugatorum*, in order to help priests be open to greater collaboration with the laity and families, recognizing their significant pastoral roles in parishes and at the diocesan level. Many local Church communities often fail to provide spouses with the possibility to assist in offering pastoral care, precisely in their identity as spouses. There is no question that the witness of families and spouses is required in order to express the missionary character of the pastoral care of marriage, alongside the specific accompaniment of pastors. In this sense, the *ecclesia docens* and *ecclesia discens* should not be separated, precisely because of the rich and concrete experience of marriage and family life which spouses possess.

Accompanying couples "in crisis"

87. In the course of every marriage, times will arise in which marital communion diminishes and spouses find themselves experiencing periods, at times lengthy, of suffering, fatigue, and misunderstandings, passing through true marital "crises." These form part of the

story of every family: "every new step along the way can help couples find new ways to happiness," making "the wine of their union" even more mature.[103]

However, in order to prevent a crisis situation from worsening to the point of becoming unsalvageable, the parish or community should offer a pastoral service for accompanying couples in crisis, to which those who perceive that they are in such a situation can turn: "What is urgently needed today is a ministry to care for those whose marital relationship has broken down."[104] Prevention of relational breakdown is a decisive factor today in avoiding separations, which can deteriorate and irreparably damage the marriage bond.

88. Experience shows that "most people in difficult or critical situations do not seek pastoral assistance, since they do not find it sympathetic, realistic, or concerned for individual cases."[105] In response, spouses who have overcome such moments of crisis should join their pastor to become "companions" for couples facing difficulties or who have already separated. They will form an "accompanying community" which bears concrete witness that the Good Samaritan is the Risen Christ, whose glorious body retains his wounds and therefore feels compassion for those who are wounded and abandoned along the roadside:[106] couples in difficulty.

89. To achieve this goal, training projects urgently need to be offered to accompanying couples who seek to assist couples in crisis or those already separated, in order to foster a pastoral service which fits the needs of

families. Attention shall be focused in two directions: to spouses in difficulty, and also to their children who must be accompanied with a psychological and spiritual perspective capable of comprehending their personal and familial distress, while offering them support.

Therefore, pastoral care of the marriage bond must accompany newly married couples even from their earliest years together as they encounter the various stages of married life. Indeed, moments of crisis form part of the marital journey, and must be transformed into opportunities, which may produce painful wounds and sores of the heart, but which always leave room for reconciliation, forgiveness, and the balm of grace, which continues to work in the sacramental bond.

90. Some crises are common in all marriages, and mark various stages of family life (arrival of the first child, childrearing, the "empty nest," ageing parents). There are also personal crises, often involving finances; problems in the workplace; emotional, social, and spiritual difficulties; or even some difficulties due to traumatic and unexpected circumstances.[107] In all these cases, "the arduous art of reconciliation, which requires the support of grace, needs the generous cooperation of relatives and friends, and sometimes even outside help and professional assistance."[108] Accompaniment in these moments, therefore, should offer both psychological and spiritual assistance, in order to rediscover the profound meaning of the marital bond and the awareness of Christ's presence among the spouses, through a personalized mystagogical path and the sacraments. When

couples fill their hearts with silence, invoke the name of Jesus Christ, and listen to his voice, they help create the conditions for God to nurture their relationship, rescue them in difficulty, and stop to drink with them from the cup of suffering, as he stands by their side like the Wayfarer with the disciples of Emmaus (see Lk 24:13).

In practical terms, this means creating privileged opportunities to introduce couples to the art of discernment in daily life, so that in times of suffering they know how to recognize the dangerous pitfalls to avoid and the immaturities or wounds to overcome. Couples whose hearts are weary can be urged to focus on the words: "Abide in my love" (Jn 15:9).

91. We suggest here, by way of illustration, one possible practical application of the principles thus far outlined, which takes the form of a spiritual program for couples in crisis inspired by Jesus' journey with the disciples of Emmaus (see Lk 24:13–35). Once the parish is appropriately acquainted with the service, couples may request to participate in the shared pathway of accompaniment. "Individual" meetings (a single couple) could be alternated with "group" meetings (involving several couples). The program could be laid out according to the following pattern:

- "Jesus himself drew near and walked with them" (Lk 24:15) — initial ("individual") meeting of welcome and acquaintance

The first meeting should take place in an environment of

confidentiality and personal closeness, thus limited to a single couple. They should be welcomed and listened to by the priest and an accompanying couple, who seek to show empathy, care, and complete availability to offer support. This first meeting of mere "listening" should be followed by others which will begin the actual accompaniment process.

- "What are you discussing as you walk along?" — several meetings ("individual") to invite the couples to tell God and their spouse why they "look downcast" (Lk 24:17)

Meetings must always be held in a prayerful atmosphere, since the couple is embarking upon a spiritual journey, not a "couples' therapy" session of counseling. The couple should therefore place themselves in God's presence and shall be guided to "open their hearts," so that each spouse becomes aware of "what makes the other suffer." The accompaniment team shall guide this "opening of the heart" so that it surpasses a simple exchange of accusations. Therefore, the couple should not be invited to answer questions like: "What mistakes have you made?" or "What should you change?" etc. Rather, they shall be asked: "What pain do I carry inside?"; "What discomfort do I feel?"; "What is it about the way we treat each other that hurts me?" Indeed, couples commonly lack opportunities to communicate and converse in such a way that allows each spouse to share their state of mind or point of view.

- "How slow of heart to believe all that the

prophets spoke! Was it not necessary that the Messiah should suffer these things and enter into his glory?" (Lk 24:25–26) — meetings ("group") with various couples to "illuminate" moments of crisis

Meetings with each individual couple may be followed by group meetings, during which one of the accompanying couples could be invited to share their experience and the crisis moments they have faced, highlighting the "new ways to happiness" they have learned in the difficulties and trials of marriage. The sessions may also include a brief teaching moment composed of a reading and commentary of appropriately chosen parts of *Amoris Laetitia,* or excerpts from the writings of saintly spouses who have overcome times of marital trial. The purpose of these group meetings is to highlight that "crisis moments" — when accepted, understood, lived together, and assisted by the Lord's help — can prove to be moments of grace and growth for the couple. Ultimately, crises are not "anomalies" but "normal" parts of married life, even those crises resulting from frailty or personal sin. These moments can also become the "afflictions of Christ" who is present with the spouses and who is wounded by their sins and suffers with them, but who enters with them into the glory (see Lk 24:26) of a healed and "redeemed" relationship. As already emphasized in the catechumenal pathway to marriage, these meetings must contain a proclamation of the kerygma: the Lord is present and living in our midst! Together with him, even the "death" of a crisis can be transformed into resurrection and new life!

- "Then beginning with Moses and all the prophets, he interpreted to them what referred to him in all the scriptures" (Lk 24:27) — meetings ("group") focused on Scripture

The previous meetings for "catechesis" may be followed by other group meetings in which couples celebrate a Liturgy of the Word together: a biblical passage is proclaimed, followed by moments of meditation and then sharing guided by a few questions, and concluding with a final reflection offered by the accompanying team. Care shall be taken to choose biblical texts exploring themes such as the nearness of God in trials, God's forgiveness which is received then shared with others, grace working in weakness, communion of hearts as a gift of the Holy Spirit, the call to holiness, the Sacrament of Matrimony, etc.

- "Stay with us, for it is nearly evening" (Lk 24:29) — Eucharistic Adoration and Sacrament of Reconciliation

A "Eucharistic evening" (or even more than one) could be offered to couples taking part in the journey. Even after a series of meetings to illuminate ongoing moments of crisis, couples often still find themselves helpless to overcome the crisis. The challenges seem beyond their strength. Perhaps this is the time to bring a particular crisis to the Lord in the Blessed Sacrament, to "present it" and "lay it" at his feet, so that he may heal the couple's wounds and hearts. This presentation of the crisis to the Lord could be expressed through a concrete gesture made by the couple before the Blessed Sacrament (offering of an object as a symbol), within a simple liturgical context.

Another way for couples to experience the Lord who "stays with us" could be through a penitential celebration. Reception of the Sacrament of Reconciliation is of supreme importance in times of crisis. Nothing helps couples heal wounds and forgive their spouse like forgiveness received from the Lord. The sacrament infuses the soul with special graces of reconciliation: reconciliation with God, one's self and one's past, and with one's neighbor. This process helps heal divisions and "inner" estrangement between spouses with the balm of reconciliation and forgiveness.

- "He took bread, said the blessing, broke it, and gave it to them" (*Lk* 24:30) — Eucharistic celebration

Couples could be invited to one or more Eucharistic celebrations to help them experience that Jesus is alive and present even in the midst of crisis. It is he who always becomes "bread broken for us" and who has experienced the suffering of rejection and misunderstanding, turning it into an occasion of love and self-giving for all. Couples may also receive this grace, so as not to remain closed in their own pain, but to turn it into an opportunity for deeper love and renewed mutual self-giving.

- "With that their eyes were opened and they recognized him. So, they set out at once and

returned to Jerusalem" (Lk 24:31, 33) — conclusion of the journey

Couples may also be invited to enjoy moments of relaxation and celebration together. Even in crises, we should never lose hope or abandon ourselves to a negative outlook on life. Above all, trust and joy can be rekindled in our hearts when we realize that we have brothers and sisters in the faith who remain close to us and support us.

The concluding meetings of the journey could help couples to "return to Jerusalem," in other words, to continue in married life with a new wisdom acquired in crisis, while putting to good use what has been learned and becoming witnesses for other couples of the experience and encounter with the risen Jesus.

These meetings, however, should not be viewed as a final leave-taking. Life always presents new challenges, and a crisis may not be fully overcome. Therefore, the accompanying team should assure couples of their continued readiness to welcome, listen to, and support them in the future. Once a climate of trust has been established, couples should continue to have someone they can turn to in times of need. The accompanying team should make couples feel that the Church is always there for them, like a mother ever ready to welcome her children.

It bears repeating that throughout the course of this program individual meetings with each couple may need to be held, in addition to group meetings. There are times when great help and encouragement can be drawn from listening to the experiences of others — as can occur in moments of sharing. At other times couples may feel the need for a more personal encounter or greater confidentiality, in order to feel free to talk about their trials.

92. The aforementioned model merely provides an example to demonstrate ways in which a program to accompany couples in crisis can recall the style of the catechumenal method of marriage preparation laid out above. Here again, the methodology should not be limited to offering "lectures" or transmitting ideas, but should foster an experience of human and spiritual closeness involving the Christian community while alternating moments of exploring the Faith with moments of meeting, prayer, listening, sharing, ritual gestures, and celebration of the sacraments. Couples should be assisted along a journey of progressive growth and invited to discernment, all in the key of a kerygmatic proclamation. Each local Church shall therefore seek to create its own catechumenal approach, with its own ways of progressing, even drawing inspiration from "biblical models" which might differ from those proposed here — the Samaritan's encounter with the man wounded by robbers (see Lk 10:25–37), the prodigal son who returns to his father (Lk 15:11–32), the wine which runs out and is made abundant again at the wedding in Cana (Jn 2:1–12), the Samaritan woman's encounter with Jesus and the desire for new water that slakes every thirst (Jn 4:1–43), along with others.

93. Despite all the support the Church offers to couples

in crisis, there remain some situations in which separation is inevitable. "At times it even becomes morally necessary, precisely when it is a matter of removing the more vulnerable spouse or young children from serious injury due to abuse and violence, from humiliation and exploitation, and from disregard and indifference." Even so, "separation must be considered as a last resort, after all other reasonable attempts at reconciliation have proved vain."[109] In these cases, "special discernment is indispensable for the pastoral care of those who are separated, divorced, or abandoned. Respect needs to be shown especially for the sufferings of those who have unjustly endured separation, divorce, or abandonment, or those who have been forced by maltreatment from a husband or a wife to interrupt their life together. To forgive such an injustice that has been suffered is not easy, but grace makes this journey possible. Pastoral care must necessarily include efforts at reconciliation and mediation, through the establishment of specialized counselling centers in dioceses."[110]

94. At the same time, "divorced people who have not remarried, and often bear witness to marital fidelity, ought to be encouraged to find in the Eucharist the nourishment they need to sustain them in their current state of life. The local community and pastors should accompany these people with solicitude, particularly when children are involved."[111] Few parishes offer them pastoral care. On the other hand, their particular situation, nurtured by the gift of fidelity to the Sacrament of Matrimony, may bear witness and offer an example for young couples, as well as for priests, to discover and

"see" in their lives the constant presence of Christ the Bridegroom, who is faithful even in solitude and abandonment. Their solitude is thus "filled" with the Lord's intimacy and their bond with the Church community, which draws near to them as a companion along the road. The nuptial dimension of the two vocations — holy orders and marriage — is manifested in these cases in all its beauty and complementarity. In this sense, the Church needs to discover the ability of separated faithful to offer pastoral care, since they can play meaningful roles in their communities by coming to the aid of others.

Conclusion

The "pastoral guidelines" offered here, though not intended to be exhaustive, seek to provide an aid and stimulus for dioceses/eparchies and parishes in developing their own "catechumenal pathways for married life," according to the indications of Pope Francis. By way of conclusion, therefore, we should recall the pastoral principles which inspired this document and which should also form the basis for the implementation documents to be developed in the particular Churches.

The primary driving principle of this document is the desire to offer couples a better and more thorough preparation for marriage. These guidelines seek to achieve that goal through a sufficiently broad approach inspired by the baptismal catechumenate, which allows them to receive an adequate formation for Christian married life, starting from an experience of faith and an encounter with Jesus. The method is therefore not limited to a few meetings in proximity to the celebration, but rather is structured to help couples perceive the "permanent" nature of the pastoral care of married life which the Church intends to carry out.

The task of accompanying couples is the duty of the entire ecclesial community, which embarks on a journey shared by priests, Christian spouses, and pastoral workers. Married couples themselves — who vary in age and years of married life — are the primary agents of this pastoral care, as they offer their experience to assist those who participate in the catechumenal journey. Ongoing formation for all is therefore needed to fulfill this goal, especially for priests, so that those in need of assistance perceive the indispensable complementarity and co-responsibility shared by the lay faithful and priests/religious engaged in family ministry.

The catechumenal pathway for married life should be considered a "pastoral tool" to be employed with discernment, wisdom, and common sense, so that it can be flexibly adapted in its means and times of implementation to encounter the concrete situations of couples, while accounting for the skills and availability of the local church's pastoral workers.

The catechumenal approach is not limited to the communication of doctrinal content, and seeks to surpass the classic form of "marriage courses." Therefore, the approach employs the catechetical method in conjunction with dialogue with couples, personalized meetings, liturgical moments of prayer and celebration of the sacraments, rituals, group meetings for couples participating in the program, assistance of external experts, retreats, and the involvement of the entire Church community, which supports the lengthy process of marriage preparation.

At all phases and stages, the catechumenal approach should always retain its kerygmatic nature. The initial proclamation of the Faith should return at each new stage, as if marking successive waves, to recall that the

Sacrament of Matrimony is "good news" — that is, it is God's gift to couples who wish to live their love to the fullest.

Each phase of the catechumenal approach holds together the journey of human growth (forming a harmonious and grounded personality; overcoming immaturity, closures, and fears; [addressing] relational dynamics of each spouse and the couple, communication skills, etc.) and the journey of spiritual growth (acceptance of God's love; personal conversion; overcoming moral limitations; prayer life; comprehension of the importance of community and the ecclesial dimension of faith; reception of the sacraments; etc.).

The catechumenal pathway for couples and young people seeks to be inserted in contemporary reality, and should not hesitate to address topics and issues which challenge contemporary culture: forming an authentic love which surpasses fragile emotional experiences; recognizing the richness and complementarity of males and females; formation in affectivity and sexuality; identifying the value of definitive choices and the human, spiritual, and social value of the family; bioethical issues; etc. In this way, the itinerary assists couples in forming a personal moral conscience and the formulation of a common family life project.

The stages of growth which the catechumenal method proposes are marked by rituals — in those places where cultural realities permit and as long as no equivocal interpretation of them is possible — to provide a conscious awareness that each step along the way becomes a turning point to draw couples further along the path, both regarding human and spiritual maturity and regarding their decision to marry, while always remaining focused on the goal of Christian married life.

The catechumenal method is divided into three major phases: remote preparation, which embraces childhood and youth ministry; an intermediate reception phase; and, the actual catechumenal phase, which in turn includes three distinct stages — a first stage of proximate preparation, which lasts longer but varies in length; a second stage of final preparation, which is more brief; and a third stage of accompaniment during the first years of married life, which concludes with the couple's inclusion in the ordinary family ministry of their parish and diocese/eparchy.

The method aims to begin from childhood to unite the discovery of the Christian Faith and initiation into the sacraments with the discovery of a vocation to marriage or priesthood/religious life.

At the same time, the widespread presence of cohabiting couples with children seeking to marry in the Church requires local communities to create programs focused on the lived experience of these couples, which run parallel to the developmental form of vocational pastoral care proposed herein. These couples undoubtedly deserve special care and attention in relation to engaged couples who already have some experience of Christian life.

The catechumenal approach offers a personalized pastoral accompaniment based above all on the testimony of the accompaniment team and other married couples involved in the program. It seeks to lead every couple to a serious personal discernment, so that the celebration of marriage and married life are the fruit of a conscious decision, which is freely and joyfully embraced, and not simply the passive acceptance of a cultural tradition or social formality.

While preparing couples for the Sacrament of Matrimony, the catechumenal approach also seeks to initiate them into ecclesial life and help them experience the Church as a place where they can nurture their marriage bond, especially through the sacraments, and where they can continue to grow in their vocation of service to others throughout their lives, thus fully developing their marital identity and ecclesial mission.

Special attention, therefore, must be given to the accompaniment of married couples in crisis. Indeed, each local church urgently needs to create a pastoral ministry dedicated to couples whose marital relationship has broken down or faces great difficulties. This service should be correlated with a pastoral ministry of reconciliation and mediation to safeguard the marriage bond and prevent separations wherever possible.

Although the feat of creating such a lengthy formative itinerary may seem unattainable, we urge particular Churches to be courageous and embrace a faith-filled perspective, recalling Jesus' teaching that the works of the Kingdom always begin as a small mustard seed, but that in time they can become large trees offering shelter and protection to those in need. By offering younger generations a catechumenal journey of growth toward marriage, the Church shall meet head-on the urgent need to accompany young people toward the fulfillment of what remains one of their greatest "dreams" and among the main goals they set out to achieve in life: to establish with the person they love a firm relationship upon which to build a family.

Let us entrust this mission to the intercession of Saint Joseph, spouse of the Virgin and Guardian of the Redeemer, and to the Blessed Virgin Mary, mother of Jesus and mother of the Church, so that they may fill us with love for all families of the world and inexhaustible zeal to work in their service.

Notes

INTRODUCTION

1. "I would like to stress the need for a 'new catechumenate' for marriage preparation. Welcoming the support of the fathers of the last Ordinary Synod, it is urgent to effectively implement what has already been proposed in *Familiaris Consortio* (66). Namely, just as the catechumenate is part of the sacramental process for the baptism of adults, so too may the preparation for marriage form an integral part of the whole sacramental procedure of marriage, as an antidote to prevent the increase of invalid or inconsistent marriage celebrations" (Francis, Address on the Occasion of the Inauguration of the Judicial Year of the Tribunal of the Roman Rota, January 21, 2017; cf. also Address on the Occasion of the Inauguration of the Judicial Year of the Tribunal of the Roman Rota, January 29, 2018; Francis, apostolic exhortation *Amoris Laetitia*, 205–11).

2. Pontifical Council for the Family, *Preparation for the Sacrament of Marriage*, May 13, 1996.

3. "Different communities will have to devise more practical and effective initiatives that respect both the Church's teaching and local problems and needs" (*Amoris Laetitia*, 199).

4. Francis, *Address to the Officials of the Tribunal of the Roman Rota for the Inauguration of the Judicial Year,* January 21, 2017.

GENERAL GUIDELINES

1. The expression appears in various studies on the subject, including F. Coudreau, in *Verkündigung und Glaube. Festgabe* für F. X. Arnold (Freiburg, Germany: Herder, 1958) and Bernhard Häring, *Sociology of the Family* (Rome: Mercier Press, 1959). Since the 1960s, some bishops' conferences also mentioned it in several na-

tional and regional documents. In addition, the apostolic exhortation *Familiaris Consortio* already marked the stages of the itinerary for marriage preparation, starting from the analogy with the baptismal catechumenate: remote, proximate, final, and subsequent accompaniment of the spouses (cf. 66).

2. "I wish to recommend the commitment of a *marriage catechumenate*, intended as an indispensable itinerary for young people and couples aimed at reviving their Christian conscience, sustained by the grace of the two sacraments, baptism and marriage. As I have explained on other occasions, the catechumenate is unique in itself since it is baptismal — that is, rooted in baptism and, at the same time, in life it must assume a permanent character — as the *grace* of the Sacrament of Matrimony is permanent" (Francis, *Address on the Occasion of the Inauguration of the Judicial Year of the Tribunal of the Roman Rota*, January 29, 2018).

3. Basil of Cesarea, *De baptism* I,1.

4. "It is necessary ... to make preparatory programs for the Sacrament of Matrimony ever more effective, not only for human growth, but above all of for the faith of the engaged couples. The fundamental objective of the encounters is to help engaged couples realize a progressive integration into the mystery of Christ, in the Church and with the Church. This carries a progressive maturation in the Faith, through the proclamation of the Word of God, adhesion to and generously following Christ" (Francis, *Address on the Occasion of the Inauguration of the Judicial Year of the Tribunal of the Roman Rota*, January 21, 2017).

5. "God, who called the couple 'to' marriage, continues to call them 'in' marriage" (John Paul II, *Familiaris Consortio*, 51).

6. "They do not need to be taught the entire catechism or overwhelmed with too much information. Here, too, 'it is not great knowledge but rather the ability to feel and relish things interiorly that contents and satisfies the soul.' Quality is more important than

quantity, and priority should be given along with a renewed proclamation of the kerygma to an attractive and helpful presentation of information that helps couples live the rest of their lives together with 'great courage and generosity'" (*Amoris Laetitia*, 207).

7. The Christian community itself is called to become involved in the preparation of engaged couples for marriage, which is an ecclesial mission. Indeed, those couples "can help renew the fabric of the whole ecclesial body" (*Amoris Laetitia*, 207).

8. "Both short-term and long-term marriage preparation should ensure that the couple do not view the wedding ceremony as the end of the road, but instead embark upon marriage as a lifelong calling based on a firm and realistic decision to face all trials and difficult moments together" (*Amoris Laetitia*, 211).

9. "In virtue of the Sacrament, [spouses] are invested with a true and proper mission, so that, starting with the simple ordinary things of life they can make visible the love with which Christ loves his Church and continues to give his life for her" (*Amoris Laetitia*, 121).

10. "Three or four meetings in the parish church cannot be defined as 'marriage preparation.' ... The preparation must be mature, and it takes time. It is not a formality: It is a Sacrament. But it must be prepared with a true catechumenate" (Francis, *Catechesis on the Commandments, 11/A: "Do not commit adultery,"* October 24, 2018).

11. Cf. *Amoris Laetitia*, 203; *Catechism of the Catholic Church*, 1632.

12. Cf. Acts 18:1–3; 18:18–19; 18:26; Rom 16:3–5; 1 Cor 16:19.

13. "This catechumenate is principally entrusted to you, parish priests, indispensable collaborators of the bishops. I encourage you to implement it despite the difficulties you may encounter" (Francis, *Address to Participants in the Course on the Marriage Process,* February 25, 2017).

14. "Priests, especially parish priests, are the first interlocutors of young people who wish to form a new family and wed in the Sacrament of Matrimony. The support of the ordained minister will

help the future spouses to understand that marriage between a man and a woman is a sign of the spousal union between Christ and the Church, helping them to become aware of the profound meaning of the step they are about to take" (Francis, *Address to Participants in the Diocesan Formation Course on Marriage and Family Promoted By the Tribunal of the Roman Rota*, September 27, 2018).

15. "Today more than ever, this preparation is presented as a true and proper occasion for the evangelization of adults and, often, of the so-called distant ones. There are, indeed, numerous young people for whom the approach of the wedding is an opportunity to encounter once again the faith which has long been relegated to the margins of their lives; moreover, they experience a unique moment, often characterized by a readiness to reexamine and change the direction of their life. ... It can be, therefore, an advantageous time for renewing their encounter with the person of Jesus Christ, with the message of the Gospel, and with the teaching of the Church" (Francis, *Address on the Inauguration of the Judicial Year of the Tribunal of the Roman Rota*, January 21, 2017).

16. "Holy Christian couples ... are the work of the Holy Spirit, who is always the protagonist of the mission, and they are already present in our territorial communities. ... Let us think about pastoral care as a catechumenate before and after marriage. These are the couples that should do it and move forward." (Francis, *Address to the Tribunal of the Roman Rota for the Inauguration of the Judicial Year*, January 25, 2020).

17. "Pastoral ministry in a missionary key seeks to abandon the complacent attitude that says: 'We have always done it this way.' I invite everyone to be bold and creative in this task of rethinking the goals, structures, style, and method of evangelization in their respective communities. A proposal of goals without an adequate communal search for the means of achieving will inevitably prove illusory" (Francis, apostolic exhortation *Evangelii Gaudium*, 33).

18. Cf. International Theological Commission, *Synodality in the Life and Mission of the Church*, March 2, 2018, 6.

19. *Amoris Laetitia*, 206.

20. "Family and young people cannot be two parallel sectors of the pastoral care of our communities, but they must walk closely together, because very often young people are that which a family has given them in their period of growth. This perspective recomposes in a unitary fashion a vocational ministry attentive to expressing the face of Jesus in its many aspects" (Francis, *Address at the Meeting with the Faithful During the Visit to Loreto*, March 25, 2019).

II. A CONCRETE PROPOSAL

1. Francis, *Address to Participants in the Course on the Marriage Process*, February 25, 2017.

2. Cf. *Amoris Laetitia*, 204.

3. "Remote preparation begins in early childhood, in that wise family training which leads children to discover themselves as being endowed with a rich and complex psychology and a with particular personality with their own strengths and weaknesses. It is the period when esteem for all authentic human values is instilled, both in interpersonal and social relationships, with all that this signifies for the formation of character, for the control and right use of one's inclinations, for the manner of regarding and meeting people of the opposite sex. ... Also necessary, especially for Christians, is solid spiritual and catechetical formation that will show that marriage is a true vocation and mission. ... Upon this basis there will subsequently and gradually be built up the proximate preparation" (*Familiaris Consortio*, 66); cf. also Pontifical Council for the Family, *Preparation for the Sacrament of Marriage*, 22.

4. The pastoral subsidy prepared by the Pontifical Council for the Family can be of great help in this task: *Human Sexuality: Truth and Meaning. Educational Orientations in the Family*, December 8, 1995.

5. "The choice of a civil marriage or, in many cases, of simple cohabitation, is often not motivated by prejudice or resistance to a sacramental union, but by cultural or contingent situations. ... Simply to live together is often a choice based on a general attitude opposed to anything institutional or definitive; it can also be done while awaiting more security in life (a steady job and steady income). In some countries, de facto unions are very numerous, not only because of a rejection of values concerning the family and matrimony, but primarily because celebrating a marriage is considered too expensive in the social circumstances. As a result, material poverty drives people into de facto unions" (*Amoris Laetitia*, 294).

6. *Amoris Laetitia*, 280, citing *Gravissimum Educationis*, 1.

7. "Marriage requires preparation, and this calls for growing in self-knowledge, developing the greater virtues, particularly love, patience, openness to dialogue and helping others. It also involves maturing in your own sexuality, so that it can become less and less a means of using others, and increasingly a capacity to entrust yourself fully to another person in an exclusive and generous way" (Francis, apostolic exhortation *Christus Vivit*, 265).

8. John Paul II, *Letter to Families (Gratissimam Sane)*, 16.

9. "Only to the extent that love is grounded in truth can it endure over time, can it transcend the passing moment and be sufficiently solid to sustain a shared journey. If love is not tied to truth, it falls prey to fickle emotions and cannot stand the test of time. True love, on the other hand, unifies all the elements of our person and becomes a new light pointing the way to a great and fulfilled life. Without truth, love is incapable of establishing a firm bond; it cannot liberate our isolated ego or redeem it from the fleeting moment in order to create life and bear fruit" (Francis, encyclical *Lumen Fidei*, 27).

10. Cf., *Christus Vivit*, 242.

11. Cf. Ibid., 206.

12. "The importance of the virtues needs to be included. Among these, chastity proves invaluable for the genuine growth of love between persons. In this regard, the synod fathers agreed on the need to involve the entire community more extensively" (*Amoris Laetitia,* 206).

13. Cf. Lk 4:40: "And he laid his hands on *each one* and healed them."

14. "With the help of missionary families, the couple's own families and a variety of pastoral resources, ways should also be found to offer a remote preparation that, by example and good advice, can help their love to grow and mature. Discussion groups and optional talks on a variety of topics of genuine interest to young people can also prove helpful. All the same, some individual meetings remain essential since the primary objective is to help each to learn how to love this very real person with whom he or she plans to share his or her whole life. Learning to love someone does not happen automatically, nor can it be taught in a workshop just prior to the celebration of marriage. For every couple, marriage preparation begins at birth. … Pastoral initiatives aimed at helping married couples to grow in love and in the Gospel of the family also help their children, by preparing them for their future married life" (*Amoris Laetitia,* 208).

15. "The faithful love of Christ is the light by which to live the beauty of human affection. Indeed, our sentimental dimension is *a call to love* that is manifested in fidelity, in welcoming, and in mercy" (Francis, *Catechesis on the Commandments, 11/B: "In Christ our spousal vocation finds fullness,"* October 31, 2018).

16. "Faith transforms the whole person precisely to the extent that he or she becomes open to love. Through this blending of faith and love we come to see the kind of knowledge which faith entails, its power to convince and its ability to illumine our steps. Faith knows because it is tied to love, because love itself brings enlightenment. Faith's understanding is born when we receive the immense

love of God which transforms us inwardly and enables us to see reality with new eyes" (*Lumen Fidei*, 26).

17. "The pastoral workers and persons in charge ... as educators, will also have to be capable of welcoming the engaged, whatever their social and cultural extraction, intellectual formation, and concrete capacities may be." (Pontifical Council for the Family, *Preparation for the Sacrament of Marriage*, 43).

18. "On the lips of the catechist the first proclamation must ring out over and over: 'Jesus Christ loves you, he gave his life to save you, and now he is living at your side every day to enlighten, strengthen, and free you.' ... All Christian formation consists of entering more deeply into the kerygma, which is reflected in and constantly illumines, the work of catechesis, thereby enabling us to understand more fully the significance of every subject which the latter treats. It is the message capable of responding to the desire for the infinite which abides in every human heart" (Francis, apostolic exhortation *Evangelii Gaudium*, 164–5).

19. Cf. *Amoris Laetitia*, 201.

20. Cf. *Familiaris Consortio*, 68; *Amoris Laetitia*, 1, 59, 200–1.

21. "The most persuasive testimony of the blessing of Christian marriage is the good life of the Christian spouses and of the family. There is no better way to speak of the beauty of the sacrament!" (Francis, *General Audience*, April 29, 2015).

22. In this effort to understand, it is helpful to consider people's subjective and objective difficulties, as well as the "difficulties of understanding" and "difficulties of living" what the Church proposes, in light of the criteria stated in *Amoris Laetitia* (301–3).

23. "At the same time, reach out in the Gospel way by meeting and welcoming those young people who prefer to live together without being married. On the spiritual and moral level, they are among the poor and the little ones, towards whom the Church, following in the footsteps of her Master and Lord, seeks to be a mother who does

not abandon but draws near and takes care of them. These people are also loved by the heart of Christ. Look to them with compassion and tenderness" (Francis, *Address to Participants in the Course on the Marriage Process*, February 25, 2017).

24. Regarding this fundamental aspect, which cannot be disregarded in order to engender an adequate renewal of pastoral care for marriage preparation, great help can be found in the document *The Reciprocity between Faith and Sacraments in the Sacramental Economy* produced by the International Theological Commission, which received Pope Francis' favorable opinion on December 19, 2019.

25. "All these situations require a constructive response seeking to transform them into opportunities that can lead to the full reality of marriage and family in conformity with the Gospel. These couples need to be welcomed and guided patiently and discretely. This is how Jesus treated the Samaritan woman (cf. Jn 4:1–26): He addressed her desire for true love, in order to free her from darkness in her life and bring her to the full joy of the Gospel" (*Amoris Laetitia*, 294).

26. *Familiaris Consortio*, 68.

27. Cf. John Paul II, Address on the Occasion of the Inauguration of the Judicial Year of the Tribunal of the Roman Rota, January 30, 2003; Benedict XVI, *Address on the Occasion of the Inauguration of the Judicial Year of the Tribunal of the Roman Rota*, January 26, 2013; Francis, Address on the Occasion of the Inauguration of the Judicial Year of the Tribunal of the Roman Rota, January 23, 2015.

28. "It is worth clearly reiterating that the essential component of matrimonial consent is not the quality of one's faith, which according to unchanging doctrine can be undermined only on the plane of the natural (cf. CIC, Canon 1055 § 1 and 2). Indeed, the *habitus fidei* is infused at the moment of baptism and continues to have a mysterious influence in the soul, even when faith has not been developed and

psychologically speaking seems to be absent. It is not uncommon that couples are led to true marriage by the *instinctus naturae* and at the moment of its celebration they have a limited awareness of the fullness of God's plan. Only later in the life of the family do they come to discover all that God, the Creator and Redeemer, has established for them. A lack of formation in the Faith and error with respect to the unity, indissolubility, and sacramental dignity of marriage invalidate marital consent only if they influence the person's will (cf. CIC, Canon 1099). It is for this reason that errors regarding the sacramentality of marriage must be evaluated very attentively" (Francis, *Address on the Occasion of the Inauguration of the Judicial Year of the Tribunal of the Roman Rota*, January 22, 2016).

29. "The traditional doctrine of the sacraments includes the conviction that the sacrament requires at least the intention to do what the Church does: All these sacraments are realized by three elements: of things, as matter; of words, as form; and of the person of the minister who confers the sacrament with the intention of doing what the Church does (*cum intentione faciendi quod facit Ecclesia*). If one of them is missing, the sacrament is not performed. According to the common opinion of Latin theology, the ministers of the Sacrament of Matrimony are the spouses, who reciprocally donate their marriage. In the case of sacramental marriage, at least the intention to perform a natural marriage is required. Now, natural marriage, as the Church understands it, includes as essential properties indissolubility, fidelity, and ordering to the good of the spouses and the good of the offspring. Therefore, if the intention to enter into marriage does not include these properties, at least implicitly, there is a serious lack of intention, capable of calling into question the very existence of natural marriage, which is the necessary basis for sacramental marriage" (International Theological Commission, *The Reciprocity of Faith and Sacraments in the Sacramental Economy*, 168).

30. "The sacramental intention is never the result of automatism, but always of a conscience illuminated by faith, as the result of a combination of the human and the divine. In this sense, spousal union can be said to be true only if the human intention of the spouses is oriented to what Christ and the Church want" (Francis, *Address on the Occasion of the Inauguration of the Judicial Year of the Tribunal of the Roman Rota*, January 29, 2018); "When in spite of all efforts, engaged couples show that they reject explicitly and formally what the Church intends to do when the marriage of baptized persons is celebrated, the pastor of souls cannot admit them to the celebration of marriage. In spite of his reluctance to do so, he has the duty to take note of the situation and to make it clear to those concerned that, in these circumstances, it is not the Church that is placing an obstacle in the way of the celebration that they are asking for, but themselves" (*Familiaris Consortio*, 68).

31. "In fact, the faith of the person asking the Church for marriage can exist in different degrees, and it is the primary duty of pastors to bring about a rediscovery of this faith and to nourish it and bring it to maturity. But pastors must also understand the reasons that lead the Church also to admit to the celebration of marriage those who are imperfectly disposed" (*Familiaris Consortio*, 68).

32. "Christian spouses are not naive; they know life's problems and temptations. But they are not afraid to be responsible before God and before society. ... Of course, it is difficult! That is why we need the grace, the grace that comes from the sacrament! The Sacraments are not decorations in life. ... Grace is not given to decorate life but rather to make us strong in life giving us the courage to go forward! ... Christians celebrate the Sacrament of Matrimony because they know they need it! They need it to stay together and to carry out their mission as parents. *In joy and in sorrow, in health and in sickness.*" (Francis, *Address to Families on Pilgrimage to Rome in the Year of Faith*, October 26, 2013).

33. "In marriage preparation courses it is indispensable to re-read the *catechesis of the Christian initiation into the Faith*, whose content must not be taken for granted or as if already known by the engaged couples. On the contrary, more often than not the whole Christian message is to be rediscovered by those who have come to a halt at some elementary notion of the catechism of first Communion or, if all goes well, that of confirmation" (Francis, *Address to Participants in the Diocesan Formation Course on Marriage and Family Promoted by the Tribunal of the Roman Rota*, September 27, 2018).

34. "The path of preparation for marriage should be implemented ... also by focusing on the essentials: the Bible, by consciously rediscovering it together; prayer, in its liturgical dimension, but also in 'domestic prayer,' to live out in the home; the sacraments; the sacramental life, confession ... where the Lord comes to abide in the engaged couple and prepare them truly to receive one another 'with the grace of Christ.'" (Francis, *General Audience*, May 27, 2015).

35. "The decision to 'wed in the Lord' also entails a missionary dimension, which means having at heart the willingness to be a medium for God's blessing and for the Lord's grace to *all*. Indeed, Christian spouses participate *as spouses* in the mission of the Church. ... The Church, in order to offer to all the gifts of faith, hope, and love, needs the courageous fidelity of spouses to the grace of their sacrament! The People of God need their daily journey in faith, in love, and in hope, with all the joys and the toils that this journey entails in a marriage and a family" (Francis, *General Audience*, May 6, 2015); see also *Familiaris Consortio*, 50; *Amoris Laetitia*, 121.

36. "The Fathers also spoke of the need for specific programs of marriage preparation aimed at giving couples a genuine experience of participation in ecclesial life and a complete introduction to various aspects of family life" (*Amoris Laetitia*, 206).

37. *Amoris Laetitia*, 296–97.

38. "There are a number of legitimate ways to structure programs of marriage preparation, and each local Church will discern how best to provide a suitable formation without distancing young people from the sacrament. ... It should be a kind of 'initiation' to the Sacrament of Matrimony, providing couples with the help they need to receive the sacrament worthily and to make a solid beginning of life as a family" (*Amoris Laetitia*, 207).

39. "Engagement ... is the time when the two are called to perform a real labor of love, an involved and shared work that delves deep. Here they discover one another little by little, [that is,] the man "learns" about woman by learning about *this* woman, his fiancée; and the woman "learns" about man by learning about *this* man, her fiancé. Let us not underestimate the importance of this learning: It is a beautiful endeavor, and love itself requires it" (Francis, General Audience, May 27, 2015).

40. Cf. *Amoris laetitia*, 133–41.

41. "The proximate preparation, which from the suitable age and with adequate catechesis, as in a catechumenal process, involves a more specific preparation for the sacraments, as it were, a rediscovery of them. This renewed catechesis of young people and others preparing for Christian marriage is absolutely necessary in order that the sacrament may be celebrated and lived with the right moral and spiritual dispositions. The religious formation of young people should be integrated, at the right moment and in accordance with the various concrete requirements, with a preparation for life as a couple. This preparation will present marriage as an interpersonal relationship of a man and a woman that has to be continually developed, and it will encourage those concerned to study the nature of conjugal sexuality and responsible parenthood, with the essential medical and biological knowledge connected with it. It will also acquaint those concerned with correct methods for the education of children and will assist them in gaining the basic

requisites for well-ordered family life" (*Familiaris Consortio*, 66); cf. also Pontifical Council for the Family, *Preparation for the Sacrament of Marriage*, 35.

42. Cf. Pontifical Council for the Family, *Preparation for the Sacrament of Marriage*, 36.

43. "The timely preparation of engaged couples by the parish community should also assist them to recognize eventual problems and risks. In this way, they can come to realize the wisdom of breaking off a relationship whose failure and painful aftermath can be foreseen. In their initial enchantment with one another, couples can attempt to conceal or relativize certain things and to avoid disagreements; only later do problems surface. For this reason, they should be strongly encouraged to discuss what each expects from marriage, what they understand by love and commitment, what each wants from the other and what kind of life they would like to build together. Such discussions would help them to see if they in fact have little in common and to realize that mutual attraction alone will not suffice to keep them together. Nothing is more volatile, precarious, and unpredictable than desire. The decision to marry should never be encouraged unless the couple has discerned deeper reasons that will ensure a genuine and stable commitment" (*Amoris Laetitia*, 209).

44. The *ius connubii* (right to marry) is not a "subjective claim that pastors must fulfill through a merely formal recognition independent of the effective content of the union. The right to contract marriage presupposes that the person can and intends to celebrate it truly, that is, in the truth of its essence as the Church teaches it. No one can claim the right to a nuptial ceremony. Indeed, the *ius connubii* refers to the right to celebrate an authentic marriage. The *ius connubii* would not, therefore, be denied where it was evident that the fundamental requirements for its exercise were lacking, namely, if the required capacity for marriage were patently lacking

or the person intended to choose something which was incompatible with the natural reality of marriage" (Benedict XVI, *Address at the Inauguration of the Judicial Year of the Tribunal of the Roman Rota*, January 22, 2011).

45. "'There is a need to accompany with mercy and patience the eventual stages of personal growth as these progressively appear,' making room for 'the Lord's mercy, which spurs us on to do our best.'" (*Amoris Laetitia*, 308); cf. also 295.

46. *Amoris Laetitia*, 300.

47. "In no way must the Church desist from proposing the full ideal of marriage, God's plan in all its grandeur: 'Young people who are baptized should be encouraged to understand that the Sacrament of Matrimony can enrich their prospects of love and that they can be sustained by the grace of Christ in the sacrament and by the possibility of participating fully in the life of the Church.' A lukewarm attitude, any kind of relativism, or an undue reticence in proposing that ideal, would be a lack of fidelity to the Gospel and also of love on the part of the Church for young people themselves. To show understanding in the face of exceptional situations never implies dimming the light of the fuller ideal, or proposing less than what Jesus offers to the human being. Today, more important than the pastoral care of failures is the pastoral effort to strengthen marriages and thus to prevent their breakdown" (*Amoris Laetitia*, 307).

48. "The importance of the virtues needs to be included. Among these, chastity proves invaluable for the genuine growth of love between persons" (*Amoris Laetitia*, 206); "Chastity is freedom from possessiveness in every sphere of one's life. Only when love is chaste, is it truly love. A possessive love ultimately becomes dangerous: it imprisons, constricts, and makes for misery. God himself loved humanity with a chaste love; he left us free even to go astray and set ourselves against him. The logic of love is always the logic of freedom" (Francis, apostolic letter *Patris Corde*, 7).

49. "A faithful and courageous education in chastity and love as self-giving must not be lacking. Chastity is not a mortification of love, but rather a condition for real love. In fact, if the vocation to married love is a vocation to self-giving in marriage, one must succeed in possessing oneself in order to be able to truly give oneself" (Pontifical Council for the Family, *Preparation for the Sacrament of Marriage*, 24).

50. "'People should cultivate [chastity] in the way that is suited to their state of life. Some profess virginity or consecrated celibacy which enables them to give themselves to God alone with an undivided heart in a remarkable manner. Others live in the way prescribed for all by the moral law, whether they are married or single.' Married people are called to live conjugal chastity; others practice chastity in continence. ... Those who are *engaged to marry* are called to live chastity in continence. They should see in this time of testing a discovery of mutual respect, an apprenticeship in fidelity, and the hope of receiving one another from God. They should reserve for marriage the expressions of affection that belong to married love. They will help each other grow in chastity" (*CCC* 2349–50).

51. "Yes, many couples are together a long time, perhaps also in intimacy, sometimes living together, but *they don't really know each other*. It seems curious, but experience shows that it's true. Therefore, engagement needs to be reevaluated as a time of getting to know one another and sharing a plan" (Francis, General Audience, May 27, 2015).

52. Cf. **CCC** 2348–50.

53. Cf. *Book of Blessings, Roman Rite* (USA 1989), 202, 212.

54. "A promise of marriage ... which is called an engagement, is governed by the particular law established by the local bishops' conference, after it has considered any existing customs and civil laws" (*CIC*, Canon 1062).

55. Cf. *Book of Blessings*, 198.

56. "In the case of the family, the weakening of these bonds is particularly serious because the family is the fundamental cell of society, where we learn to live with others despite our differences and to belong to one another; it is also the place where parents pass on the Faith to their children. Marriage now tends to be viewed as a form of mere emotional satisfaction that can be constructed in any way or modified at will. But the indispensable contribution of marriage to society transcends the feelings and momentary needs of the couple. As the French bishops have taught, it is not born 'of loving sentiment, ephemeral by definition, but from the depth of the obligation assumed by the spouses who accept to enter a total communion of life'" (*Evangelii Gaudium*, 66).

57. Cf. Pontifical Council for the Family, *Preparation for the Sacrament of Marriage*, 45–46.

58. "The final preparation for the celebration of the Sacrament of Matrimony should take place in the months and weeks immediately preceding the wedding" (*Familiaris Consortio*, 66).

59. The content of these talks should become the object of explicit catechesis, so that, when they take place, the couple approaches them not as a mere formality but as an important moment of free acceptance of marital commitments and full assumption of responsibility. In this regard, the following words of Benedict XVI should be kept in mind: "Among the means of ascertaining whether the project of the engaged couple is truly conjugal, the pre-matrimonial examination stands out. This examination has a mainly juridical purpose: to ascertain that [which] impedes the valid and licit celebration of the wedding. However juridical does not mean formal, as though it were a bureaucratic step, like filling up a form based on set questions. Instead it is a unique pastoral opportunity — one to be made the most of with the full seriousness and attention that it requires — in which, through a dialogue full of respect and cordiality, the pastor seeks to help the person to face seriously

the truth about himself or herself and about his or her own human and Christian vocation for marriage. In this sense the dialogue, always conducted separately with each of the engaged pair without lessening the possibilty of further conversations with the couple, requires an atmosphere of full sincerity in which stress should be put on the fact that the contracting parties themselves are those first concerned and first obliged in conscience to celebrate a valid marriage" (Benedict XVI, *Address on the Occasion of the Inauguration of the Judicial Year of the Tribunal of the Roman Rota*, 22 January 2011).

60. Cf. *Amoris Laetitia*, 59–66.

61. Cf. *CCC* 1606–8.

62. "The celebration of this sacrament acquires special significance for family life. While they discover in faith that sin contradicts not only the covenant with God, but also the covenant between husband and wife and the communion of the family, the married couple and the other members of the family are led to an encounter with God, who is 'rich in mercy' (Eph 2:4), who bestows on them his love which is more powerful than sin, and who reconstructs and brings to perfection the marriage covenant and the family communion" (*Familiaris Consortio*, 58).

63. "In their preparation for marriage, the couple should be encouraged to make the liturgical celebration a profound personal experience and to appreciate the meaning of each of its signs. In the case of two baptized persons, the commitment expressed by the words of consent and the bodily union that consummates the marriage can only be seen as signs of the covenantal love and union between the incarnate Son of God and his Church. In the baptized, words and signs become an eloquent language of faith. ... At times, the couple does not grasp the theological and spiritual import of the words of consent, which illuminate the meaning of all the signs that follow. It needs to be stressed that these words cannot be reduced to

the present; they involve a totality that includes the future" (*Amoris Laetitia*, 213–4).

64. "The sacrament is not a 'thing' or a 'power,' for in it Christ himself 'now encounters Christian spouses.' ... Christian marriage is a sign of how much Christ loved his Church in the covenant sealed on the cross, yet it also makes that love present in the communion of the spouses. By becoming one flesh, they embody the espousal of our human nature by the Son of God. ... Even though the analogy between the human couple of husband and wife, and that of Christ and his Church, is 'imperfect,' it inspires us to beg the Lord to bestow on every married couple an outpouring of his divine love" (*Amoris Laetitia*, 73).

65. "What comes to mind is the miracle of the multiplication of the loaves: for you, too, the Lord can multiply your love and give it to you fresh and good each day. He has an infinite reserve! He gives you the love that stands at the foundation of your union, and each day he renews and strengthens it. And he makes it ever greater when the family grows with children" (Francis, *Address to Engaged Couples Preparing for Marriage*, February 14, 2014).

66. Cf. *CCC* 1624: "In the epiclesis of this sacrament the spouses receive the Holy Spirit as the communion of love of Christ and the Church. The Holy Spirit is the seal of their covenant, the ever-available source of their love and the strength to renew their fidelity." See also *Amoris Laetitia*, 120. The Rite of Marriage includes several epicleses; we will just mention some of them (according to the Italian version of the *editio typica altera* of the *Ordo Celebrandi Matrimonium* approved by the Congregation for Divine Worship and the Discipline of the Sacraments by Decree Prot. no. 874/02/L of 29 April 2004): the prayer at the end of the invocations of the saints: "Pour out, O Lord, upon N. and N. the Spirit of your love, that they may become one heart and one soul: Let nothing separate these spouses whom you have joined together, and, filled with your bless-

ing, let nothing afflict them. Through Christ our Lord"; The epiclesis within the prayer of blessing of the spouses (first formula): "Look now with kindness on these your children who, united in the bond of marriage, ask the help of your blessing: pour upon them the grace of the Holy Spirit so that, by the power of your love effused in their hearts, they may remain faithful to the conjugal covenant"; In the prayer of blessing of the spouses (second formula): "O God, stretch forth your hand upon N. and N. and pour into their hearts the power of the Holy Spirit. Grant, O Lord, that, in the union consecrated by you, they may share the gifts of your love and, becoming for each other a sign of your presence, be one heart and one soul."

67. Cf. *CCC* 1622; Pontifical Council for the Family, *Preparation for the Sacrament of Marriage*, 53.

68. Cf. Pontifical Council for the Family, *Preparation for the Sacrament of Marriage*, 50–58.

69. "Christian marriage preparation can be described as a journey of faith, which does not end with the celebration of marriage but continues throughout family life. Therefore, our perspective does not close with marriage as an act, at the moment of celebration, but as a permanent state" (Pontifical Council for the Family, *Preparation for the Sacrament of Marriage*, 16).

70. "Pastoral care is most effectively realized where the *accompaniment* doesn't end with the wedding, but 'escorts' at least the first years of conjugal life. Through conversations with the individual couple and moments in community, young spouses can be helped to acquire the instruments and the support for living their vocation. And this cannot occur but through a path of growth in the faith of the couples themselves" (Francis, *Address to Participants in the Diocesan Formation Course on Marriage and Family Promoted by the Tribunal of the Roman Rota*, September 27, 2018).

71. "It is all the more essential that couples be helped during the first years of their married life to enrich and deepen their conscious

and free decision to have, hold and love one another for life. Often the engagement period is not long enough, the decision is precipitated for various reasons and, what is even more problematic, the couple themselves are insufficiently mature. As a result, the newly married couple need to complete a process that should have taken place during their engagement" (*Amoris Laetitia*, 217).

72. "The covenant of love between man and woman — a covenant for life — *cannot be improvised*. It isn't made up one day to the next ... one needs to work on love, one needs to walk. The covenant of love between man and woman is something learned and refined. I venture to say it is a covenant carefully crafted. To make two lives one is almost a miracle of freedom and the heart entrusted to faith" (Francis, *General Audience*, May 27, 2015).

73. "Their union is real and irrevocable, confirmed and consecrated by the Sacrament of Matrimony. Yet in joining their lives, the spouses assume [with Jesus present in their midst] an active and creative role in a lifelong project. ... By saying 'I do,' they embark on a journey that requires them to overcome all obstacles standing in the way of their reaching the goal. The nuptial blessing that they receive is a grace and an incentive for this journey. They can only benefit from sitting down and talking to one another about how, concretely, they plan to achieve their goal" (*Amoris Laetitia*, 218).

74. "Especially in the first five years of married life, it would be desirable to follow up the young couples through post-marriage courses, to be carried out in parishes or deaneries" (Pontifical Council for the Family, *Preparation for the Sacrament of Marriage*, 73).

75. See, for example, Cyril of Jerusalem, *Mystagogical Catecheses*; Ambrose of Milan, *De Sacramentis* and *De Mysteriis*.

76. Cf. *Amoris Laetitia*, 133–5; 143–6; 163–4; 321–3.

77. Cf. Ibid., 125; 147–52; 319–20.

78. Cf. Ibid., 77; 120–4.

79. Cf. Ibid., 72–75; 317–8.

80. "The common life of husband and wife, the entire network of relations that they build with their children and the world around them, will be steeped in and strengthened by the grace of the sacrament. For the Sacrament of Matrimony flows from the Incarnation and the Paschal Mystery, whereby God showed the fullness of his love for humanity by becoming one with us. Neither of the spouses will be alone in facing whatever challenges may come their way. Both are called to respond to God's gift with commitment, creativity, perseverance, and daily effort. They can always invoke the assistance of the Holy Spirit who consecrated their union, so that his grace may be felt in every new situation that they encounter" (*Amoris Laetitia*, 74).

81. "Their gaze now has to be directed to the future that, with the help of God's grace, they are daily called to build. For this very reason, neither spouse can expect the other to be perfect. Each must set aside all illusions and accept the other as he or she actually is: an unfinished product, needing to grow, a work in progress. A persistently critical attitude towards one's partner is a sign that marriage was not entered into as a project to be worked on together, with patience, understanding, tolerance, and generosity. Slowly but surely, love will then give way to constant questioning and criticism, dwelling on each other's good and bad points, issuing ultimatums and engaging in competition and self-justification. The couple then prove incapable of helping one another to build a mature union. This fact needs to be realistically presented to newly married couples from the outset, so that they can grasp that the wedding is 'just the beginning'" (*Amoris Laetitia*, 218).

82. Cf. *Amoris Laetitia*, 221.

83. Cf. Ibid., 106; 163; 210; 232–4; 240.

84. "This process occurs in various stages that call for generosity and sacrifice. The first powerful feelings of attraction give way to

the realization that the other is now a part of my life. The pleasure of belonging to one another leads to seeing life as a common project, putting the other's happiness ahead of my own, and realizing with joy that this marriage enriches society" (*Amoris Laetitia*, 220).

85. "As love matures, it also learns to 'negotiate.' Far from anything selfish or calculating, such negotiation is an exercise of mutual love, an interplay of give and take, for the good of the family. At each new stage of married life, there is a need to sit down and renegotiate agreements, so that there will be no winners and losers, but rather two winners" (*Amoris Laetitia*, 220).

86. "Young married couples should be encouraged to develop a routine that gives a healthy sense of closeness and stability through shared daily rituals. These could include a morning kiss, an evening blessing, waiting at the door to welcome each other home, taking trips together, and sharing household chores" (*Amoris Laetitia*, 226).

87. Cf. *Amoris Laetitia*, 17–18.

88. Cf. Ibid., 313ss.

89. Cf. Ibid., 150–7.

90. Cf. Ibid., 80–83.

91. Cf. Ibid., 84–85; Francis, *General Audience*, May 20, 2015.

92. "Couples who have learned how to do this well can share some practical suggestions which they have found useful: planning free time together, moments of recreation with the children, different ways of celebrating important events, shared opportunities for spiritual growth. They can also provide resources that help young married couples to make those moments meaningful and loving, and thus to improve their communication" (*Amoris Laetitia*, 225).

93. Cf. *Amoris Laetitia*, 211.

94. "Couples should be helped to realize that surmounting a crisis need not weaken their relationship; instead, it can improve,

settle and mature the wine of their union. ... When marriage is seen as a challenge that involves overcoming obstacles, each crisis becomes an opportunity to let the wine of their relationship age and improve" (*Amoris Laetitia*, 232).

95. "Spousal spirituality ... should therefore include regaining the dynamism of sacraments, with a special role of the Sacraments of Reconciliation and the Eucharist. The Sacrament of Reconciliation glorifies divine mercy toward human misery and makes the vitality of baptism and the dynamism of confirmation grow. From this the pedagogy of redeemed love is strengthened which lets the greatness of God's mercy be discovered before the drama of man, created by God, and wonderfully redeemed. By celebrating the memory of Christ's giving to the Church, the Eucharist develops the affective love proper to marriage in daily giving to one's spouse and children, without forgetting and overlooking that 'the celebration which gives meaning to every other form of prayer and worship is found in *the family's actual daily life together*, if it is a life of love and self-giving' (*EV*, 93)." (Pontifical Council for the Family, *Preparation for the Sacrament of Marriage*, 41).

96. Cf. *Amoris laetitia*, 186; 318.

97. Cf. Ibid., 105–8.

98. Cf. Ibid., 227–9.

99. Cf. Francis, *Address to the Tribunal of the Roman Rota for the Inauguration of the Judicial Year*, January 29, 2019.

100. Cf. *Amoris Laetitia*, 313–324; Francis, apostolic exhortation *Gaudete et Exsultate*, 14–34.

101. Cf. Ibid., 87.

102. Cf. Ibid., 88; 324.

103. Cf. Ibid., 232. On the challenge of marital crises, cf. nos. 232–40.

104. Cf. Ibid., 238.

105. Cf. Ibid., 234.

106. Cf. Francis, *Audience with Members of the "Retrouvaille"
Association*, November 6, 2021.
107. Cf. *Amoris Laetitia,* 235–236.
108. Cf. Ibid., 236.
109. Cf. Ibid., 241.
110. Cf. Ibid., 242.
111. Ibid.